RECLAIMING THE GOSPEL AT HOME:

BIBLICAL TRUTHS FOR MEN

Charles A. Fowler, Editor

innovo
PUBLISHING

Published by
Innovo Publishing LLC
www.innovopublishing.com
1-888-546-2111

Providing Full-Service Publishing Services for
Christian Authors, Artists & Organizations: Hardbacks, Paperbacks,
eBooks, Audiobooks, Music & Film

RECLAIMING THE GOSPEL AT HOME: BIBLICAL TRUTHS FOR MEN

Library of Congress Control Number: 2014904033
ISBN 13: 978-1-61314-188-5

Cover Design & Interior Layout: Innovo Publishing, LLC

Printed in the United States of America
U.S. Printing History

First Edition: January 2014

Dedicated

To the faithful members of Germantown Baptist Church.
I am blessed to be serving and shepherding you as your pastor.

To Sandra,
a precious gift from God.
I am blessed to be sharing my life with you as your husband.

To Anna and Sarah,
daily reminders of God's grace and goodness.
I thank God for allowing me the privilege of loving
and caring for you as your father.
You are a joy!

For group leader resources,
personal study extras, and
practical "how to" conversations
for reclaiming the gospel in our homes, visit
reclaimingthegospelathome.org.

Follow us on Twitter at @gospelathome
Like us on Facebook at facebook.com/gospelathome

TABLE OF CONTENTS

FOREWORD

I was sitting recently at the funeral of a man who died only weeks after his doctors discovered an inoperable brain tumor. As his son walked behind the pulpit to eulogize this minister, I pondered how difficult, emotionally, it would be to do this. The son, though, calmly said that many people had asked him about his esteemed father, wondering, "What was he like at home?" This son said, "You all saw him. You heard him preach and teach. He was the same at home as the man you knew and admired, and that's why I not only love him but respect him too."

That testimony is all too rare. We're all hypocrites because we're all sinners. Our lives don't measure up to our ideals; our testimonies don't measure up to our theologies. If we say otherwise, the Bible tells us, we're deceiving and being deceived.

But our fallenness doesn't consign us to a life of failure and defeat. Through the gospel, the blood of Christ stands between our accuser's threats and us. And through the gospel, the Spirit of Christ inhabits and enlivens us. This gospel dynamism isn't just about what happens in our prayer closets or in our work lives but also about what happens at our dinner tables, in our living rooms, and on our deathbeds.

This book, made available by one of the most faithful pastors I know, is a good tool to point us all to God's purpose for gospel-driven homes. Rooted in the life of our forefather David, the book points us to what it means to live a life of integrity, powered by our hope and trust in David's descendant, our Lord Jesus.

I was convicted by this book to reflect more deeply on what it means to pour my life into my five sons in a way that points them to the gospel I hold. Read this book and ask what it would mean for you to see yourself as your children or grandchildren would see you. It might change what's said around the table at your house tonight. And it might change what's said, one day, at your funeral.

Russell D. Moore
President, Ethics & Religious Liberty Commission
Southern Baptist Convention

ACKNOWLEDGMENTS

This book has been a collaborative process. One of the unique blessings afforded me has been the opportunity to view the entire process from beginning to end. This vantage point has allowed me to see the Body of Christ work together with great synergy to see the vision for providing biblical truth applied to real life and spiritual encouragement to men become a reality. While I cannot acknowledge everyone, it is important to mention those, who without their personal investment, this project might not have been completed. They are Ronald Meeks, Travis Fleming, Justin Wainscott, Cliff Pace, Jim Collier, Chuck Herring, Trent Bullock, Todd Brady, Ashley Ray, Mike Priest, Greg McFadden, and Matt Surber. These men made time in their busy schedules that are already filled with family and ministry priorities to contribute chapters to this *Reclaiming the Gospel at Home* project. Thank you!

In addition, there were several who assisted in the editorial process. Their thoughtful and detailed service has made an invaluable contribution to this overall project. I cannot say thank you enough for their passionate pursuit of excellence that has enabled this book to communicate much more effectively than would have been the case without their expertise. They are Dottie Weir, Brenda Doss, Jane Brown, and Francis Haynes.

The GBC Communication Team has worked with me and in cooperation with the professionals at Innovo Publishing to develop logos to support this project and promotional strategies to let churches know of this new resource. I am grateful for their time and creative contribution.

This acknowledgment page would be incomplete without expressing heartfelt appreciation for the vision, professionalism, and godly character demonstrated by Bart Dahmer and the entire team at Innovo Publishing.

My hope-filled prayer is that God will take this book and use it to be a blessing to families and churches as it provides biblical insight to men who want to be men "after God's own heart." Proverbs 11:25 states, ". . . he who waters will himself be watered." As each of these have given liberally of their time, wisdom, and biblical insight to shepherd this *Reclaiming the Gospel at Home* project, I pray that the spiritual refreshment that is delivered to men through this book will be rewarded by God releasing the refreshing waters of His Spirit in the lives of those who helped make this vision come to fruition.

INTRODUCTION

The life of David provides distinctive insight into the process through which God shapes a "man after His own heart." Scriptures provide great detail about most of his life. The biblical account provides windows into his life beginning with his early days as a shepherd boy who was growing in his understanding of God's purpose for life and being equipped to walk in it. We have a window into his home life. We see David as a husband, father, and grandfather who, at times, provided a faithful example but at other times walked through intense spiritual, emotional, and relational battles within his family. Thankfully, Scripture also allows us to see his public life as a leader of God's people. David stood tall during some difficult times. He demonstrated grace under pressure and provided us an example of being a true worshipper of God. It is a great blessing that we are afforded such insight into the making of a man of God.

Many men desire to grow into mighty men of faith whose hearts reflect God's great love. Unfortunately, for too many, life simply gets in the way and spiritual priorities get lost among the challenges we face. David faced many similar problems. We see him struggling with adultery, murder, and lies. We see him losing his throne, facing public ridicule, and dealing with rebellious children. Throughout his roller-coaster life, we see a man who always returned to the moorings of his faith. He provides a model of repentance, worship, and faith. Since life for men today is filled with triumph and failure, there is much we can learn from David's example. We see God's faithfulness expressed through his life in such powerful ways that it should serve as an encouragement to men today that God's love is true, tenacious, and forgiving.

As we consider David's life, we see a multitude of adversities that he faced. Some were of his own making while others were situations he simply encountered through the flow of his life. As we observe the effect of these adversities, it is evident that as David grew older and had the benefit of many encounters with God, his character became more consistent and reflective of the heart of God. God used those difficult seasons of life to shape David's heart in much the same way a potter shapes clay. While David was walking through those times, we see the impact of the stress and anxiety they produced in his life. Thankfully, as we pull back and view the overall impact of those difficulties, we can only marvel at how God redeemed them for good and produced the man of God whose example provides us wisdom and encouragement.

When we examine the biblical examples of his unfaithful decisions, there is an often-unnoticed aspect of David's life from which we should draw encouragement. It is the spiritual reality that his sin and unfaithfulness did not paralyze him. It appears that when he stepped outside of God's call for his life, he repented, sought forgiveness, and moved on to acts of faithfulness. He embraced God's ability to transform his life through those often painful and costly situations. There is no indication that he felt disqualified from pursuing God's purpose and presence in His life nor is there cause to think he felt irrevocably damaged by his sin. God was gracious to provide us a picture of biblical transformation and restoration. Was David's sin ugly and painful? Yes. Was the power of God to transform and restore him on the other side of repentance demonstrated? Absolutely! God was always faithful to David, and He continues to be faithful with us today, even in response to sin and a repentant heart. David trusted Him and walked that path to restoration and renewed purpose many times. Thankfully, God provides a path for all of us to be renewed spiritually and experience His power, which enables us to live a consistently transformed life.

The chapters in this book are written by pastors. The pastoral perspective on the challenges faced by men today is unique and important. For many men, when their lives become chaotic and challenging, they turn to their pastors for prayer and biblical counsel. This allows pastors to gain insight into the decisions that set the stage for adversity as well as the path of biblical truth that leads to transformation. Just as God used shepherding as a tool to help equip David for his life's purpose, learning from the wisdom gained by those who shepherd our church families provides distinctive insight and hope for men who desire spiritual growth and vitality.

The path to experiencing God's transformation is a path paved by the Word of God. The Scriptures are true. The Holy Spirit takes that truth and applies it with great precision in the lives of those seeking wisdom, discernment, and transformation. Therefore, each chapter in this book draws from the rich source of the Word of God for direction. When Scripture speaks and we obey, our lives are changed. Hopefully, as the truths of God's Word are exposed through this book, each reader will learn that these are indeed truths that transform!

Each of the pastors contributing to this *Reclaiming the Gospel at Home* project joined me in praying that God uses this book to encourage greater faithfulness in our men, which will result in stronger, healthier homes. Stronger homes will help strengthen churches. Ultimately, God created us to live in community with God, with our families, and with our church families. That is why He established the nature of the church to be a family of families.

Men have a distinctive leadership role in the home. As we grow in consistent faithfulness, our influence at home will encourage our families to grow in consistent faithfulness. As husbands and fathers, we must learn to embrace our spiritual responsibility of being the primary disciplers of our families, regardless of the challenges we face. In fact, the real need for families is to see husbands and fathers who continually and consistently pursue God even when the circumstances of life provide us excuses for neglecting the call of God upon our lives. Every man, like David, is called as a young man to pursue God's purpose and prepare to embrace it. We are called to be godly husbands and fathers, and we are called to walk publicly with an overtly expressed faith that is seamless when transitioning from personal life to family life to public life. God gives us the ability through the truths of His Word applied by the Spirit of God to live such a consistently obedient life.

For His Glory,
Charles A. Fowler

1

WALKING BY FAITH IN GOD'S DECLARED PURPOSE

INTRODUCTION

"God has a plan, a place, and a purpose for every life." Dr. Wilfred Tyler of Blue Mountain College wrote these words on the black board and explained them to students on the first day of class each year. God wants all people to discover and fulfill His plan for their lives. At a crucial time in the history of Israel, God declared His purpose to a young boy who would impact all of subsequent history.

This particular Old Testament story began with an unpleasant trip for Samuel to Bethlehem. He journeyed to Bethlehem, the "house of bread," to anoint a new king—a replacement for Saul whom he had previously anointed. Perhaps as he traveled, he thought about Saul's successful start—a great victory, a celebrative coronation, and rallying point for the people of Israel. But inevitably, his mind likely turned to Saul's downfall—unwise decisions, foolish oaths, and rebellious acts. His heart was grieving over Saul, but perhaps this soon-to-be anointed new king would give the people a fresh start.

When he arrived at Bethlehem, the people were anxious. They wondered if they had committed some trespass that warranted a visit from the best-known spiritual leader of the day for the purpose of offering a sacrifice on their behalf. Soon they learned that the visit was a peaceful one, maybe the most important visit ever made to Bethlehem up to that time.

Samuel called Jesse and his family to the ceremony, not to simply be spectators, but vital participants. He listened to the voice of God to identify and anoint His chosen king of Israel. Eliab stepped before him, but Samuel had ears for the voice of God and heard Him say, "Do not look at his appearance or his stature, because I have rejected him. Man does not see what the LORD sees, for man sees what is visible, but the LORD sees the heart" (1 Samuel 16:7). Samuel was swift to listen. Saul too had been a striking figure, a head taller than any other man, but his height was not the measure of the inner man or an indication of how high he might rise spiritually. The Lord said He rejected Eliab. Samuel continued to listen attentively and look carefully to anoint the one the Lord indicated to him. Then the next son came, and the next, and the next, until an entire procession of Jesse's sons had paraded before Samuel. When the cavalcade of young men finally ceased, no one had been anointed.

Samuel asked, "Are these all the sons you have?"

"There is still the youngest," answered Jesse. Jesse explained that the youngest was out caring for the sheep. He was doing the job his father had given him to do.

"Send for him. We will not sit down until he gets here," declared Samuel.

So they sent for David. Someone took the message and yelled out to him in the field, "David, come quickly! Jesse needs you—now!" All that is described about David was the outward appearance. He had beautiful eyes and a healthy, handsome appearance. It was not the outward appearance, however, that was the consideration; it was the heart. The Lord spoke to Samuel, "Anoint him, for he is the one." Without hesitation, Samuel opened the horn and poured the holy anointing oil upon David. If you had been there, you could have seen it flowing over his head, over his face, and over his clothes, and you could have smelled the fragrant aroma drifting through the air. Perhaps you would have thought, *This is a special moment.* This anointing was powerfully symbolic because the Spirit of the Lord "took control" of David from that day forward. He was called and anointed for His high service. He was a shepherd boy—and king of the people of God. However, at least seventeen years would pass before God's declared purpose in David's life would be fulfilled.

God has a purpose for every life. He is constantly working in the lives of His people to reveal His purpose and to empower His people to fulfill His purpose. Sometimes, as in the case of David, many years pass and many challenges are experienced before God's plan is accomplished in its fullness. What can be learned from considering David's journey that provides hope and encouragement to others pursuing a faithful expression of God's will in their own lives?

TRIALS

Faith is required to persevere in the Lord's service when one understands his or her purpose, but has yet to see it come to pass. One faces many circumstances and tests, which try the breadth and depth of that faith. David experienced a number of tests between the time he was anointed by Samuel in Bethlehem and the time he was anointed as king of Israel. One challenge came from within his own family as his brother Eliab, who was the first to be passed over at the anointing, objected to David's entrance into the battle against Goliath (1 Samuel 17:28). He implied that as a boy, David should be home taking care of the sheep instead of meddling in the military affairs.

Another challenge was David's encounter with Goliath. The impending battle appeared to be the mismatch of all mismatches. David was younger, smaller, and more inexperienced than the huge, battle-savvy Goliath. Through his faith in the Lord, the boy from Bethlehem prevailed over the giant from Gath (1 Samuel 17:50).

David also faced the continual challenge of the Philistines and other enemies in Israel, such as the Amalekites. These enemies were intent on destroying David. The Philistines had settled initially along the Mediterranean coastal region of Israel, but they steadily moved into the central hill country encroaching deeper into Israelite territory. They were a great threat to Israel, and Saul ultimately lost his life battling them (1 Samuel 31:1–13). David was able to win significant victories against them, and when he became king of Israel, he was able to strike down the Philistine forces at Baal-perazim (2 Samuel 5:23–25). The Amalekites were a nomadic tribe who were a perpetual thorn in Israel's side. Saul failed to destroy them as commanded by the Lord, but David was able to win a significant victory over them (1 Samuel 30:1–25).

However, the most significant challenges David had to overcome were the persistent attempts by Saul to destroy him. On two separate occasions, Saul personally tried to pin David to the wall with a spear. As David played the harp in an attempt to help Saul, Saul hurled the spear at David to kill him. Each time, David eluded Saul's bloodthirsty anger (1 Samuel 18:10–11, 19:9–10). Through trickery, Saul endeavored to eliminate David by arousing the anger of the Philistines. Saul promised to give his daughter, Michal, in marriage to David if he brought him one hundred Philistine foreskins. Saul thought if David met that price at the expense of the Philistines, it would enrage the Philistines against David. David brought twice the price Saul demanded, but the Philistines were not able to match the might and cunning of David (1 Samuel 18:30).

When Saul failed to eliminate David by his own personal efforts and through the Philistine trap, he sent out his troops against the future king. His orders were simple: "Kill David." His army ran after David in Ramah, but they were overcome by the Spirit of God (1 Samuel 19:19–24). Saul went after David and almost apprehended him in the Wilderness of Maon, but he had to break off his pursuit because of a Philistine invasion (1 Samuel 23:26–28). The paranoid monarch chased David to a cave in En-Gedi, and David could have killed Saul in the darkness of the cavern; however, David would not touch God's anointed (1 Samuel 24:1–15). In what was essentially his last attempt, Saul hunted David in the hill of Hachilah; but again, ironically, he almost hunted David with such careless abandon that it could have set the stage for his own demise. David and his men stood at his head while he slept with the opportunity to assassinate him (1 Samuel 26:1–24). With all his army, Saul could not apprehend God's anointed king because the Lord was with David and preserved him in all his exploits.

All believers who seek to walk in God's declared purpose and seek to fulfill God's calling in their lives will experience challenges or tests to their faith. These challenges are real threats, which have destructive potential. Peter alerted believers to the threats of the evil one when he wrote: "Be sober! Be on the alert! Your adversary, the Devil, is prowling around like a roaring lion looking for anyone he can devour. Resist him, firm in the faith, knowing that the same sufferings are being experienced by your brothers in the world" (1 Peter 5:8–9). The evil one would like to ruin Christian business leaders by entangling them in unethical practices. He would like to spoil Christian disciples through false teachings. He would like to consume Christian ministers through all types of sin. Therefore, believers must prepare themselves to overcome the challenges that confront them through authentic faith in God.

TRUTH

God Clarifies His Purpose

The study of David's pursuit of God's purpose in his life reveals at least two key truths for believers who would understand and live out God's purposes in their lives faithfully. The first truth is that God desires to clarify His purpose in the lives of His people, just as He did in the life of David. While God's calling of a person to follow Him is, in some way, unique to each individual, there are some common means in which God reveals His purposes. God clarified His purpose for David in several key ways.

First, God used a significant person in David's life to help him discover His purpose. Samuel was the outstanding religious leader of his day. He was the uniquely born, prophetically gifted, and dynamically used servant of the Lord. Samuel was divinely directed to the town of Bethlehem. When he called the sons of Jesse to the sacrifice, he rejected each one until David arrived. He anointed David, the youngest, communicating God's divine purpose for his life. God used Samuel to reveal His will for David. In addition, while it does not appear that Samuel had a continuing relationship with David, it is clear that when David was being hunted by Saul, he fled to Samuel and reported to him all that Saul had done (1 Samuel 19:18). Samuel served as both a listening ear and safe refuge for God's future king.

God still uses significant people today to clarify His purposes in the lives of others. He uses pastors, missionaries, and other church leaders to communicate His Word and will to people. He uses parents, grandparents, other relatives, and friends to help people understand God's plans. In addition, God often uses leaders in schools, such as principals, teachers, and coaches to help students find the pathway to discovering God's will.

Second, God also uses ceremony or ritual to clarify and confirm His call. It was no small thing that Samuel, the representative of God, in sacred convocation, used the holy anointing oil to set David apart as the next king of Israel. Samuel was set apart for that purpose. The people were gathered for that purpose. The oil was formulated for that purpose.

While some believers minimize the significance of ceremony, all Christian groups participate in some dramatic public ceremonies. The most universal and significant Christian ceremony is baptism. Baptism is a public confession of one's faith in Jesus Christ. The act symbolizes dramatically an individual's faith in Jesus as the crucified, buried, and risen Savior, and it pictures the death of the former person and his or her resurrection to new life. This act of obedience is mightily symbolic of God's work in the person. The ordinance is a powerful ceremony, which reminds Christ followers that Jesus is actively working in and through their lives.

There are other ceremonies practiced by Christians today. They include the observance of the Lord's Supper, wedding ceremonies, ordination services for church leaders, missionary commissioning services, dedication services for parents and children, and services solemnizing commitments to moral purity. Far from just going through a ritual, those who have entered into these highly symbolic ceremonies with a genuine desire for dedication and consecration have found them to be life-shaping experiences that honor God and encourage them to live lives true to their calling as followers of Christ.

Finally, God clarified His purpose to David by the endowment of His Spirit. The Bible states, "So Samuel took the horn of oil and anointed him in the presence of his brothers, and the Spirit of the Lord took control of David from that day forward" (1 Samuel 16:13). The Christian interpreter is careful to follow the development of God's revelation of His Spirit's work throughout the Scriptures. An analysis of the person and work of the Spirit in the Old Testament reveals that typically the Spirit of God came upon persons in the Old Testament to empower them for specific tasks but not to indwell them.[1] It is significant that the writer of 1 Samuel stated that David experienced the presence of the Spirit of God "from that day forward." The presence of the Spirit was a guiding, empowering personal force in his life.

God continues to use the Spirit in the lives of His people to clarify His purpose in their lives. Gratefully, believers are blessed with the opportunity to experience both the indwelling and empowerment of the Holy Spirit. After the bestowal of the Holy Spirit at Pentecost, fulfilling the promise of the Father, believers—young and old, male and female—

---

[1] Andrew Hill and John Walton, A Survey of the Old Testament, 3rd Ed. (Grand Rapids: Zondervan, 2009), 244.

have been privileged to experience the indwelling presence of God's Holy Spirit.

According to the New Testament, the Holy Spirit comes to reside within the individual. He regenerates (Titus 3:5), baptizes (1 Corinthians 12:13), indwells (1 Corinthians 6:19–20), and seals (Ephesians 4:30) God's redemptive work and calling for all believers. The Holy Spirit teaches believers and guides them into truth (John 14:26). His presence in believers is the sign and assurance that they are children of God (Romans 8:8–11; 1 John 3:24). Believers are encouraged to be filled with the Spirit (Ephesians 5:18), to walk in the Spirit (Galatians 5:16), and to follow the Spirit (Galatians 5:25). Believers should nurture and cherish their relationship with God's Spirit so that they do not lie to Him (Acts 5:3), grieve Him (Ephesians 4:30), or quench Him (1 Thessalonians 5:19). The Spirit is God's gift to His people and enables them to know God's mind and fulfill His purpose.

Faith is Essential for Walking in God's Purpose

A second truth is that faith in God is essential for walking in His declared purpose. To know God's purpose and yet be forced to wait for that purpose to be completed demands great faith. In David's case, he had to wait at least seventeen years for God's calling as the king of Israel to become a reality. The author of Hebrews stated the certainty of David's faith when he wrote, "And what more can I say? Time is too short to tell about Gideon, Barak, Samson, Jephthah, of David and Samuel and the prophets" (Hebrews 11:32–33). David is numbered among those included in the hall of fame of the faithful.

The books of First and Second Samuel contain several key statements reflecting David's faith in the Lord. When he sought to persuade Saul to allow him to fight and defeat Goliath, he contended, "The Lord who rescued me from the paw of the lion and the paw of the bear will rescue me from the hand of the Philistine" (1 Samuel 17:37). In the same story, when he faced Goliath, he declared boldly, "Today, the Lord will hand you over to me . . . and this whole assembly will know that it is not by sword or by spear that the LORD saves, for the battle is the LORD's. He will hand you over to us" (1 Samuel 17:46–47). David expressed supreme confidence that the Lord would give victory in the most challenging battles.

A second clear indication of David's faith in God was his obedience to the Lord's guidance in response to his prayers. When David learned that the Philistines were attacking Keilah, he asked God if he should launch an attack against the Philistines. Although David's men were afraid, upon receiving an answer from the Lord, David engaged the Philistines in battle and rescued the inhabitants of Keilah (1 Samuel 23:1–7). On another occasion, David was faced with the issue of pursuing the Amalekite raiders who had attacked the city of Ziklag and kidnapped the wives and children of David's men. Again, David asked for God's direction, and he was told to chase the hostile raiders. Obediently, David followed the Lord's instructions and ultimately overtook the Amalekite robbers, recovering all of the people and goods they had taken (1 Samuel 30:1–18). In each of these instances, David asked for the Lord's guidance and followed the Lord's directions, resulting in victory for David and glory for God.

A third clear indication of David's faith was his pattern of attributing to God the credit and the glory for the accomplishments and victories he was able to attain. On one occasion, David had the opportunity to take the life of Saul, his most determined enemy. David and his men slipped in to Saul's camp, taking Saul's spear and water jug, which were placed near his head. David wanted Saul to know that he remained loyal because if he had been disloyal, he could have killed Saul easily. He explained, "I wasn't willing to lift my hand against the Lord's anointed, even though the LORD handed you over to me today" (1 Samuel 26:23). Likewise, when the Lord gave David victory over the Amalekites, he acknowledged that the Lord had given them the plunder declaring, "He [the Lord] protected us and handed over to us the raiders who came against us" (1 Samuel 30:23b). Without fail, David demonstrated his faith in the Lord by ascribing credit to Him for each achievement.

TRANSFORMATION

Nothing is mentioned of David until 1 Samuel 16, when the youngest son of Jesse is brought into the presence of Samuel and anointed by him. But by 2 Samuel 5, David has been transformed into the king of Israel. By embracing God's purpose and walking by faith, David experienced a gradual, yet genuine, transformation. David cooperated with the Lord as He brought about this significant metamorphosis. David's actions can serve as examples of faithfulness and provide believers with a path toward transformation that can help equip them to walk in God's declared purpose for their lives today.

First, David responded obediently to God's purpose, and therefore, God shaped his heart into that of a shepherd. One of the first statements made about David was "[H]e is tending the sheep" (1 Samuel 16:3). When Saul dispatched messengers to bring David to his court, he was with the sheep (1 Samuel 16:19). When David's three older brothers were in Saul's army, David's primary responsibility at home was tending his father's flock (1 Samuel 17:15). When David appealed to Saul to let him battle Goliath, he did so on the basis of the experience he gained shepherding his father's flock (1 Samuel 17:34–37). When David was finally anointed king over Israel by the elders of Israel, they were aware of God's plan to make David a shepherd of the nation saying, "The LORD also said to you, 'You will shepherd My people and be ruler over Israel'" (2 Samuel 5:2). All of his life David had been developing the caring, protecting heart of a shepherd for God's flock.

One who walks in God's declared purpose today will have a sincere concern for the people of God. Believers acknowledge that Jesus is the Good Shepherd who has given His life for the sheep (John 10:14–15). The new commandment Jesus gave to His followers is that they would love one another just as He had loved them (John 13:34–35). The thrust of the last recorded commission of Jesus to Peter recorded in John's Gospel is "Shepherd my sheep" (John 21:15–17). The Lord, who is the Good Shepherd, loves His people and develops in them a caring heart toward others.

Second, David responded with courage. David's courageous actions were a strong contrast to those of Saul. Unfortunately for Israel, Saul was a leader who, at times, motivated others by fear and who was motivated by fear himself. When he first rallied the army of Israel, he threatened to butcher the oxen of anyone who refused to march in the army (1 Samuel 11:6). Saul sinned against the Lord by failing to destroy the sheep and oxen taken in battle with the Amalekites because he "feared the people" (1 Samuel 15:24). Even his relentless campaign to kill David was motivated by fear. Three times the writer of 1 Samuel stated that Saul was afraid of David (1 Samuel 18:12, 18:15, 18:29). David, on the other hand, acted courageously in the face of frightening situations. Fear did not hinder him from fighting his Philistine foe, Goliath, as it did the soldiers in Saul's army (1 Samuel 17:24). Fear did not deter him from waging war against the Philistine forces (1 Samuel 18:30, 23:1–7). Fear did not keep him from chasing and conquering the Amalekite raiders (1 Samuel 30:1–25). Although he fled from Saul to avoid death, even then, he trusted in the Lord to deliver him. His secret to living courageously is stated in one of his songs: "When I am afraid, I will trust in you. In God whose word I praise, in God I trust; I will not fear. What can man do to me?" (Psalms 56:3–4).

Men and women who embrace God's purpose for their lives choose, like David, to respond to life's challenges with courage instead of fear. They listen to God's encouragement when He says, "Be alert, stand firm in the faith, be brave and strong" (1 Corinthians 16:13). They rest on God's truth when He declares, "For God has not given us a spirit of fearfulness, but one of power, love, and sound judgment" (2 Timothy 1:7).

A third evidence of God's faithfulness expressed through David's life is that David shared life with his family and friends. God did not call David to exist in isolation; rather, He called him to live in community among his friends. Even though his brothers may have resented David for a time, his family came to be with David at Adullam when they needed him and when he needed them (1 Samuel 22:1). But the most notable example of David sharing life with others is his deep friendship with Jonathan, Saul's son. David and Jonathan shared a genuine loving friendship. The writer of 1 Samuel provided the following description: "When David had finished speaking with Saul, Jonathan committed himself to David, and loved him as much as he loved himself" (1 Samuel 18:1). They shared much in common, as they both were courageous warriors, they both won significant military victories, and they both possessed a profound faith in the Lord.[2] They found in each other a friend at the deepest level. David trusted Jonathan and literally put his life in Jonathan's hands (1 Kings 19:1–8). During their final documented meeting in Scripture, Jonathan rushed out to David before his father, Saul, arrived and encouraged David's faith in the Lord, reaffirming the covenant they had made on previous occasions (1 Samuel 23:14–18).[3]

---

[2] Robert D. Bergen, 1, 2 Samuel: in New American Commentary (Nashville: Broadman Press, 1996), 199.

[3] Bergen, 235.

David and Jonathan loved one another, and their lives were richer because of their deep commitment to one another.

Followers of Christ today can emulate David's example by sharing our lives with others, as God's Word calls us to do. The word *church* translated in the New Testament, *ekklesia*, means "the called out ones" and refers to the assembly of the people of God. The New Testament writers used the vivid image of the people of God as a "body" to describe the vital connection that exists among God's people (1 Corinthians 12:12–30). They added the rich metaphor of the family or "household" to describe the loving relationships among God's people (Ephesians 5:19; 1 John 5:1). In addition, the New Testament contains at least twenty-one exhortations calling believers to care for "one another" as they share life together. This is the essence of living as believers within the church.

One final observation of how God's faithfulness was expressed through David's life is seen in how David waited on God's timing. He was anointed as king by Samuel, probably as a teenager, but did not become king of Israel until about age thirty-seven. David had several opportunities to potentially seize the throne of Israel before God's appointed time. As mentioned previously, he could have killed Saul on two occasions, but he did not want to touch God's anointed ruler. Even when Saul died, David might have met with the elders of Israel at age thirty and negotiated his way to the kingship. But in truth, God had much to teach David before his rule was established. In addition, the people of Israel needed the assurance that David was God's anointed, not one who usurped the throne from Saul. Eventually, it was made clear to Saul (1 Samuel 24:20), Jonathan (1 Samuel 23:17), Abner (2 Samuel 3:18), and the elders of Israel (1 Samuel 3:17–18) that David was the rightful king.

To walk in God's declared purpose, God's servants today may also have to wait for God's timing to bring about His plan in their lives. They may have to wait like expectant parents to see the birth of a dream. Certainly all who anticipate the coming of Jesus must wait expectantly for the hour, known only by the Father, when the Son shall appear and transform believers into His likeness (1 Corinthians 1:7; 1 John 3:2).

When the Bible first introduced David, he did not appear to be special. His brothers were far more impressive in appearance than David, and his father simply identified him as the youngest. His life is proof that God delights to use "the foolish things of the world to shame the wise and has chosen to use the weak things to shame the strong" (1 Corinthians 1:27). The Lord took a humble shepherd boy and used him to change history as He accomplished His purpose in David's life.

Are you ready to see God's purpose accomplished in your life? Sir Winston Churchill, the Prime Minister of Great Britain and an exceptional leader of men, once wrote: "To every man there comes in his lifetime that special moment when he is figuratively tapped on the shoulder and offered the chance to do a very special thing, unique to him and fitted to his talent. What a tragedy if that moment finds him unprepared or unqualified for the work which would have been his finest hour."[4] Embrace God's purpose, walk by faith and in obedience, and let God work out His purpose in your life in His power and His time.

QUESTIONS FOR REFLECTION

Personal Reflection

1. When God looks upon your "heart," what do you think He sees?

2. David was anointed because Samuel listened to God's voice. What have others said to you to indicate they see God working in your life?

3. David was "under the control" of the Spirit from the time he was anointed. Does your life give evidence of the control of the Spirit? Is it possible that you might be grieving or quenching the Spirit's work in your life?

4. When God taps you on the shoulder and calls you for a purpose or task He has for you, do you think you will be prepared or unprepared for that task? Why or why not?

---

[4] As quoted in Bill L. Taylor, 21 Truths, Traditions, & Trends: Propelling the Sunday School into the 21st Century (Nashville: Convention Press, 1996), 181.

Group Reflection

1. How do baptism, the Lord's Supper, ordination, parent/child dedication, or some other ceremonies remind believers today to follow Christ?

2. In what ways have you seen Satan try to devour you or members of your church?

3. How does your church function as a community for believers where you can share your lives with one another?

4. What enabled David to be patient through the long years until God actually allowed him to wear the crown and take the throne? What enables us to be patient in our present circumstances?

Dr. Ronald T. Meeks joined the faculty of Blue Mountain College in Blue Mountain, Mississippi, in 1997 and is currently the professor of Bible and director of church relations. His primary roles are to teach the Bible and help young people prepare for the gospel ministry. Meeks serves as pastor of Unity Baptist Church in Ramer, Tennessee. He received his bachelor of arts degree with majors in Bible and English from Blue Mountain College (1983). Later, he earned his master of divinity degree in biblical studies (1986) and his doctor of philosophy degree in pastoral ministries (1996) from the New Orleans Baptist Theological Seminary. While a teenager, he felt called to preach the gospel and was licensed to the gospel ministry in 1975. Dr. Meeks is married to Julie Bertsche, and together they have three children—Matthew, Charlie, and Carolyn Grace—and one grandchild, Tristan. Ronald enjoys spending time with his wife, children, and grandchild, boating with friends and church members at the lake, and reading and studying the Bible. The Meeks make their home in Corinth, Mississippi.

2

FACING GIANTS IN FAITH

INTRODUCTION

The book of 1 Samuel provides a detailed description of a cathartic moment in David's life. How did David respond? How can teenagers, today, learn from his example and respond faithfully to their personal faith challenges and crises?

In 1 Samuel 16, the prophet Samuel is commissioned by the Lord to find a new king for the people of Israel. Samuel is told that Jesse's youngest son was out tending sheep. David made his way to meet with Samuel, and the Lord confirmed that David was the right man (1 Samuel 16:12–13).

Eventually, David became King Saul's armor bearer. In chapter 17, the plot thickens when the Philistines and the Israelites get ready for battle. Yet, this was not a battle for the Israelites where they were facing an underdog (an NCAA DIII team, one might say). The Philistines had a star on their team. He was 9' 9" (1 Samuel 17:4). To say that Goliath was intimidating would be an understatement.

He was not passive either. He taunted the Israelites, and he challenged one of their men to a fight. The Israelites were terrified (1 Samuel 17:11). Who would the Israelites send out to fight this giant, Goliath?

Goliath taunted the Israelites for forty days. Then David arrived at the Israelites' camp. He learned quickly that Goliath wanted to fight. David replied emphatically, "Just who is this uncircumcised Philistine that he should defy the armies of the living God?" (1 Samuel 17:26).

King Saul agreed to allow David to go out and fight Goliath. This set the stage for a significant and unavoidable test of David's faith.

Would he trust in his own strength, that of the Israelites, or in Yahweh's power to defeat Goliath?

Contemporary Context

Teenagers may not face literal nine-foot-plus Goliaths in their lives today, but the types of giants they face are numerous and hold equal destructive force. The enemy is out to attack from the homeroom bell on the first day of school throughout life. Teens must navigate these vitally important years in a day and age when temptations are greater than perhaps they ever have been.

Sexual promiscuity is one such giant. With MTV music presentations like Miley Cyrus performed (August 2013) and with songs by Brittany Spears (released September 2013) with an expletive in the title, teens are bombarded with poor role models like land mines peppered across a battlefield. These "role models" are painting a picture that sexual promiscuity makes one cool, successful, and accepted.

Drugs and alcohol are also giants that come knocking on teens' doors, and these giants promote a false sense of security and identity. How does one navigate such a precarious world of giants around every corner? Moreover, how does a parent find hope for his or her teen in such a post-Christian culture?

If it were not for the God of the Scriptures, there would be no hope to offer. The Gospel of Jesus Christ provides the reality of sustainable and meaningful hope. There are several proper pathways to grow in godliness and become a true man of faith. It is possible to follow Jesus while facing today's challenges and giants.

TRIALS

How is one to understand the definition of trials? The book of James is an excellent place to start. James said we should "Consider it a great joy, my brothers, whenever you experience various trials, knowing that the testing of your faith produces endurance. But endurance must do its complete work, so that you may be mature and complete, lacking nothing" (James 1:2–4). Hence, one can see that trials will occur in the life of a believer in order to test faith.

David's faith was tested when he faced Goliath, and this most likely occurred while he was a teenager. Would he run from Goliath or fight? Would he try to fight in his own strength and capability, or would he fight in the strength only God provides? Thankfully, he stepped up. Through his faith in God, he passed his test, and his relationship with God was strengthened, publicly and privately.

Far too often, adults and teenagers do not pass these faith tests. It is sad to say that unfaithfulness defines believers' lives too frequently. Let's consider some of the contemporary giants or trials that teenagers face.

Sexual Sins

David did not face sexual temptations in his fight with Goliath; however, when one looks at his life, it is apparent that he was tested in this area. Today's teenager is blasted with images through various technologies, such as television, movies, and social media. Our digital age introduces a new avenue for sexual immorality that was not around when most parents of teens were growing up. Unfortunately, for today's teen, these technologies are no longer on the periphery of society but are defining and shaping the prevalent culture in society.

Teenage believers have faced similar trials for decades. While the areas of temptations are the same, technology has made them more accessible and, therefore, more pervasive and tempting. Teens have the ability to text, Tweet, Facebook, Instagram, or download apps with their smartphones and tablets, which allow sin to be right at their fingertips. It used to be that teens had to go to the store to buy material, see something at a friend's house, or rent something from a video store, but that is simply no longer the case.[1]

---

[1] Russ Moore says, "Every generation of Christians has faced the pornography question, whether with Dionysian pagan art, or with Jazz Age fan-dancers, or with airbrushed centerfolds." Russ Moore, "What's at Stake with Internet Pornography" taken from http://www.russellmoore.com/2013/07/23/whats-at-stake-with-internet-pornography/

Usually, after being exposed to pornographic material, teenagers are drawn to experiment with sex. Sexual sin is progressive in nature. When one becomes comfortable with an area of sin, it will lead to deeper more costly sin expressions in life without repentance.

Pride

David could have become quite pompous after his defeat of Goliath. After all, no one else, not even those who were older, bigger, and stronger could defeat Goliath; however, he accomplished this as a mere shepherd boy. Although the text of 1 Samuel 17 does not tell us, one would imagine that there must have been the temptation to become prideful.

Men and women have a strong desire to be noticed, to be liked by others. This desire begins at a very young age. Even a three-year-old wants to be liked by the friends he or she is around.

By one's teenage years, there is no doubt that teens are faced with a strong desire to fit in. No one wants to be left out. The Lord created humans to dwell in community. It will either be found among the "right" crowd, or it will be sought among those in the "wrong" crowd. Nevertheless, community will be experienced.

Pride leads us to desire popularity and recognition. Whether two, sixteen, or seventy, control and influence within community is always desired. Adam and Eve had a desire to be in control, to be powerful; it did not work out too well. There is nothing wrong with desiring community (God made us that way); it is how and where we find it that matters.

Compromise

The serpent first appeared in the Garden of Eden with the lure of compromise for Eve. Teenagers are faced with the temptation to compromise in numerous areas of their lives. "Compromise with sexual behavior; no one will know," so the serpent whispers in the ear of the young lady craving affection or in the mind of the hormone-driven young man. "There is no such thing as absolute truth," says the university professor to the impressionable mind of the eighteen-year-old college freshman. Or "Jesus is just one of many ways to know truth," suggests the "popular kid" to the weak Christian whose faith is ill equipped for a defense. Compromise is around every corner. How can teenagers navigate these spiritual trials?

TRUTH

Relationship

David was able to overcome his crisis in his battle with Goliath due to his personal relationship with God. Within this relationship, God allowed him the opportunity and equipped him for success in battling predators as he tended his family's sheep. In 1 Samuel 16:13, one can see that when Samuel the prophet anointed David as king, "the Spirit of the LORD took control of David from that day forward." David's relationship enabled him to face many difficult trials, even the battle with Goliath. Everything he needed to obey God's will was provided to him through the Spirit of God. David learned to be dependent on the Spirit of God for his strength and wisdom.

Christian parents should seek to equip their children with a Christ-centered worldview. The process of discipleship begins from the time children are toddlers. Emphasize the biblical truth and certain reality that Christ loves them and pursues a relationship with them. Parents should model faithfulness to God's purpose in their own lives and help their children discover and follow God's plan and purpose for their lives as well.[2] Living a life of sustained faithfulness and obedience may seem impossible. Thankfully, God promises that His Spirit empowers us to do what is humanly impossible for His glory. Whether as a parent or as a teenager, the life of faith is a life of wholesale dependence on the Spirit of God for provision, enablement, and wisdom.

Pursuing anything that is not honoring to Christ can result in feelings of emptiness and want. One might say, "No one can understand how I feel or what I am going through!" No matter the intensity or the pain one might experience, Christ understands it all. The Scriptures reveal that Christ was tempted in every way, but He did not sin (Hebrews 4:15). Christ loves you, and He will forgive you of all your sins at the

---

[2] Augustine said that our souls are restless until they find rest in Christ. Wikiquote, "Augustine of Hippo," en.wikiquote.org/wiki/Augustine_of_Hippo

point of repentance and faith. The following verse gives the simple essence of the Gospel: "For God loved the world in this way: He gave His One and Only Son, so that everyone who believes in Him will not perish but have eternal life" (John 3:16). The "world" in this verse is not nature by itself, but God so loved "people." That is every teenager, every mom, every dad, and every human God has ever made.

Obedience

Once a relationship with Christ begins, the Lord looks for obedience from His children—from those who call Christ Lord, Savior, and Friend. David first responded with obedience by obeying his earthly father. When Samuel the prophet asked Jesse if he had any more sons, Jesse sent for David while he was in the fields tending to Jesse's sheep. Moreover, when Jesse sent for him, David did what he was told. Additionally, in 1 Samuel 17:20, one can see that David obeyed his earthly father when Jesse told him to take some food to the Israelite's military camp. He could have said he did not want to because he was too busy, but he readily complied.

The first thing teens must realize is that God has placed moms and dads as authority figures in the home to help guide them. It is in this guiding role of parents that teenagers begin seeing that parents provide guidance within the context of a deep, abiding love. Guidance is offered and followed through the lens of nurturing love.

The Scriptures clearly admonish believers to obey the Lord. Jesus said in John 14:23–24, "Jesus answered, 'If anyone loves Me, he will keep My word. My Father will love him, and We will come to him and make Our home with him. The one who doesn't love Me will not keep My words. The word that you hear is not Mine but is from the Father who sent Me.'" This passage highlights the connection between obedience and love. Direction is given in love and obeyed in love. The context for this entire relationship is love, both in the giving and the receiving.

Faith

A passive faith falls short of obedience. In fact, passive faith is an oxymoron. James gives the believer a great definition of what active faith looks like. In chapter 2:17, James points out that faith must have works: "In the same way faith, if it doesn't have works, is dead by itself." Furthermore, James states in chapter 2:24 that a person "is justified by works and not by faith alone." The action on the part of the believer shows, or acts as verification, that the person has true saving faith.[3]

David showed that he had an active faith by the fact that he did not sit back passively in his relationship with the Lord. When he first heard that Goliath wanted to fight one of the Israelites, he could have run back home crippled with fear. His fear could have been even greater when he heard that this battle was not a "three taps and you are out" type of wrestling match. Goliath was out to draw blood. He was out to make sure that his opponent was lying lifeless in the end! David's faith, however, was stronger than anything the enemy could hurl his way.

In Christ, one is more than a conqueror. Nothing can defeat the Christian who walks with the Lord Jesus in a personal relationship. Paul shared some amazing truth in Romans 8:31. It reads, "What then are we to say about these things? If God is for us, who is against us?"

Furthermore, those who are in Christ Jesus do not have to allow "snags" or "wrenches" in their lives to derail their spiritual walk. For instance, when Saul fitted David with his armor, and he tried to walk in it to no avail, David could have walked away saying that it must not have been God's will since a snag in the plans had arisen. Yet, that is not what happened at all. He knew he was supposed to fight Goliath. So he went with just his staff, slingshot, shepherd's bag, and five smooth stones in his hand (1 Samuel 17:40).

One does not have to become crippled with despair even when things might seem to go from bad to worse. David's situation was turning from bad to worse from man's point of view. How so? As David marched out to fight Goliath, it was quite obvious that Goliath was not intimidated by the sight of a young shepherd boy. It would be like putting a teenager well under six feet on the basketball court against Shaquille O'Neil. Goliath, with a mean-spirited tone, asked David, "Am I a dog that you come against me with sticks?" Then he cursed David by his gods (1 Samuel 17:43). Notice the strength of David's active faith in the very words he confidently spoke to Goliath: "You come against me

---

[3] I owe my conclusions to Douglas Moo's analysis of James in The Letter of James. The Pillar New Testament Commentary (Grand Rapids: William B. Eerdmans, 2000) 130–42.

with a dagger, spear, and sword, but I come against you in the name of Yahweh of Hosts, the God of Israel's armies—you have defied Him. Today, the Lord will hand you over to me. Today, I'll strike you down, cut your head off, and give the corpses of the Philistine camp to the birds of the sky and the creatures of the earth. Then the entire world will know that Israel has a God, and this whole assembly will know that it is not by sword or by spear that the Lord saves, for the battle is the Lord's. He will hand you over to us" (1 Samuel 17:45–47).

David had ample opportunity to flee during the heat of his battle. Goliath was larger than life standing over nine feet tall, and he was not inviting David out for a cookout or for a game of horse on the basketball court. In fact, Goliath started moving toward David (1 Samuel 17:48), but David did not retreat. Do not miss the significance of what happened next. David "ran quickly" to the battle line to face Goliath, and with one stone and the slingshot in his hand, he took out the fiercest foe the Israelites had ever met!

TRANSFORMATION

Teens are well aware of their personal giants, which have reared their ugly heads too many times. It is a victorious day when one can rejoice over defeating one of these giants, but far too often, teens lose the small skirmishes. The good news is that the battle is not lost. There is hope in Christ—for greater is He who is in us than he who is in the world (1 John 4:4). There is hope for everyone, regardless of past successes and failures. What are the elements that help prepare for victory and transformation?

Relationship

The Gospel of Jesus Christ is the first consideration when seeking victory. The reality of life is that everyone has messed up and everyone has experienced failure and dysfunction. The fall of Adam and Eve brought sin and separation from Creator God into the world (Romans 5:12). The good news of the Gospel, however, is that Jesus came into the world to make all things new. He came that we might have life and have it more abundantly (John 10:10). He came to reconcile us to God the Father (2 Corinthians 5:19). He came to put into action the most extravagant display of grace and mercy ever imagined (Ephesians 2:8–9). If one has never accepted Christ as Lord and Savior, then the first step must be to repent and believe in Christ (Mark 1:15). One will never be able to overcome his or her own personal giants alone. It is only in Christ that one will be able to have victory. Moreover, it is only when one experiences the forgiveness that Christ brings into believers' lives that one will be able to move on from the losses with the giants in one's life.

God invites us into relationship because without His continual enabling and empowerment, the enemy will plunder our lives through sin. We must acknowledge our deep need for God every day. We must take practical steps, such as seeking to be discipled by more mature believers, submitting to accountability relationships, and welcoming the influence, teaching, and encouragement of others to walk faithfully in our relationship with Christ.

Forgiveness

Even followers of Christ mess up and fall into sin. Believers lose skirmishes from time to time. The Christian, however, must realize that just because a small skirmish has been lost, the battle is not lost.

What is an appropriate response when sexual sin is experienced? How is a parent to deal with a son who falls into sexual sin? What about the teen who battles a drug or alcohol addiction? Mom and Dad, point your son or daughter to Christ and His glorious Gospel. Teenager, look to Christ and His forgiveness. The first thing that one must realize is that Christ forgives all of sin—past, present, and future. As one confesses his sin to Christ, he is able to experience the forgiveness that Christ already paid for when He died upon the cross as a substitutionary sacrifice for believers (1 John 1:9). One must start with confession and realize that Christ forgives all who ask for forgiveness.

One may say, "Well, what do I do about this guilt and shame that I am carrying around with me?" The thoughts may continue, "Surely, God must look at me differently because of my past sin." The biggest hurdle for most teens or adults who have fallen prey to sexual sins is a feeling of guilt and shame. For the teenager who struggles with any area of sexual sin, shame and guilt may overshadow one's realization of victory over lust in

Christ. For the young man or young lady who may have crossed the line sexually, guilt and shame and the enemy's constant reminder of one's lapse sexually, even if it was just a one-time thing, echoes in the mind like a loud, beating drum—a drum beat that does not allow one to realize that Christ brings forgiveness from all of our shame and guilt.

As the Holy Spirit brings conviction and an awareness of sin, and forgiveness and restoration is sought, we must realize there is no one who can ever rob the believer of Christ's forgiveness. The apostle Paul declares in Romans 8:1–2, "Therefore, no condemnation now exists for those in Christ Jesus, because the Spirit's law of life in Christ Jesus has set you free from the law of sin and of death."

Hence, we must realize, even after messing up and losing a skirmish, or perhaps even several skirmishes, that Christ has set His children free from sin and shame. The fact that Christ frees every believer from condemnation, regardless of its source, leads us to embrace the spiritual reality that believers have a new identity in Christ, which helps us strive to live like Christ and turn away from future temptations.

Identity

Jesus gives every believer a new identity. He does this by freeing the believer from the "old man" and restoring in one's life what went wrong in the Fall (2 Corinthians 5:17). In other words, Christ makes everything new. He gives new purpose, new meaning, new gifting, and new life. Many teens, as well as adults, struggle with trying to find a crowd who will accept them, and this struggle shows that the person has yet to realize his or her new identity in Christ.

The giant of peer pressure can cause one to fall prey to thinking that the craving for community can be satisfied with little or no regard for God's created plan and purpose for community. Believers who seek fulfillment of God-given desires outside of God's planned purpose for their lives will fall into sin. We must realize our new identity in Christ. First comes a personal relationship; then forgiveness from sin; and then an understanding of the new "Spirit-filled" life, a life in which the Holy Spirit enables the believer to move away from the old life and even current struggles with sin. The apostle Paul points out in his letter to the Galatians in 5:16–18 that walking in the Spirit is how one can keep from falling to struggles with sin: "I say then, walk by the Spirit and you will not carry out the desire of the flesh. For the flesh desires what is against the Spirit, and the Spirit desires what is against the flesh; these are opposed to each other, so that you don't do what you want. But if you are led by the Spirit, you are not under the law." The Holy Spirit cements our identity in Christ and allows us to faithfully express it in life.

The giant of pride pounces on teenagers and adults alike. People want to be noticed and liked by others, and if one allows such pride to drive his or her decisions, he or she will fall in the skirmish with pride. Yet, a Spirit-filled life enables the believer to recognize when there is pride present and when the desire to be liked by others might push one over the edge toward compromise, which then can lead to sin. The Holy Spirit leads believers to recognize that when one is in Christ, one desires the things of Christ more than the things of the flesh. Christ is the believer's preeminent example of what it means to have an attitude of humility and sacrifice, which is the antithesis of pride. Paul painted an amazing picture of the work of Christ and His example of humility in Philippians 2:5–11, "Make your own attitude that of Christ Jesus, who, existing in the form of God, did not consider equality with God as something to be used for His own advantage. Instead, He emptied Himself by assuming the form of a slave, taking on the likeness of men. And when He had come as a man in His external form, He humbled Himself by becoming obedient to the point of death—even to death on a cross. For this reason God highly exalted Him and gave Him the name that is above every name, so that at the name of Jesus every knee will bow—of those who are in heaven and on earth and under the earth—and every tongue should confess that Jesus Christ is Lord, to the glory of God the Father." When one realizes that our new identity in Christ calls one to a life of sacrifice, one will realize that there is no room for pursuit of self or recognition among men for one's own accomplishments. Galatians 2:20 provides a beautiful summary of this truth. It reads: "and I no longer live, but Christ lives in me. The life I now live in the body, I live by faith in the Son of God, who loved me and gave Himself for me." It is Christ "in me" that enables this life of selflessness and sacrifice. Embrace Christ and allow His life to radiate from yours.

Accountability

If we want to maintain victory over the giants that may have won skirmishes in the past, we must be willing to be held accountable by other godly men and women. The teenager who thinks he can handle the struggles with sexual temptations on his own is not living in reality.[4] God has created humans for community, and it is in the church that believers are to spur one another on toward good works. The writer of Hebrews declared in chapter 10:24: "And let us be concerned about one another in order to promote love and good works." Additionally, Paul wrote in 1 Thessalonians 5:11, "Therefore encourage one another and build each other up as you are already doing." Onc cannot shun accountability if one wants to remain in a place of restoration and healthy Christian living. It is through accountability with other Christian friends and mentors that one can find strength and encouragement to remain faithful to Christ. It is when one becomes "unequally yoked" with the wrong set of friends that one will be tempted to give in to sin.[5]

Prayer

Prayer by no means is to come last in the list of priorities for a believer's life. Yet, consider prayer to be interwoven in every step in the process of transformation. Prayer is to be something that is done, as the apostle Paul said in 1 Thessalonians 5:17, "without ceasing." The New Living Translation says it well, "Never stop praying." The Lord should not be a last resort in a believer's life—certainly not when facing giants to which we may have succumbed to in the past.

Prayer, if misunderstood, can seem like another homework assignment to the teen who despises another monotonous duty on his to-

---

[4] For an excellent chapter on how to relate to teenagers on sex, see chapter 28, "Teenagers and Sex." Jay Kesler, ed., with Ronald A. Beers, Foreword by Billy Graham, Parents & Teenagers: A Guide to Solving Problems and Building Relationships (Wheaton: Victor Books, 1984).

[5] I gleaned some insight for this paragraph from the following website: http://www.allaboutgod.com/christian-accountability.htm

do list before bedtime. A teenager should learn to walk in relationship with Christ so intimately that he talks with Him as he would a close friend.

Furthermore, Christian author and professor Bryan Chapell gives a solid definition of prayer for the believer in his book, *Praying Backwards*. He points out that praying with constant and specific prayers is like having an "unbroken conversation of the soul with God in a life of perpetual worship."[6] What an amazing picture! Prayer then can be seen as an "unbroken conversation of the soul." When the giants are approaching, or even during the middle of a confrontation when it seems like we may lose a skirmish, turn to Christ in fervent prayer—and keep on praying to the One who has won the victory over sin! Romans 6:12 admonishes us to "not let sin reign in your mortal body, so that you obey its desires." Romans 6:14 concludes by stating, "For sin will not rule over you, because you are not under law but grace." God, through Christ, gives us the ability to overcome sin's temptation and sin's debilitating consequences. Parents, you must let your children know that they are constantly being prayed for by you and by others. Also, you should articulate answered prayers to illustrate God's continued working in your life as an example to your children. Walk intimately with God through prayer and experience this sustainable, victorious lifestyle.

QUESTIONS FOR REFLECTION

Personal Reflection

1. What giants do you wrestle with in your life (either currently or in the past)?

2. Do you carry guilt or shame in your spiritual walk for past skirmishes you have lost? Why or why not?

---

[6] Bryan Chapell, Praying Backwards: Transform Your Prayer Life By Beginning In Jesus' Name (Grand Rapids: Baker Books, 2005) 108.

3. How have you been able to find victory over your personal giants?

4. What plans do you have in place to make sure you can remain victorious over your personal giants?

Group Reflection

1. What are some of the possible giants that teenagers face today from which they must be diligent to guard themselves in their spiritual journeys?

2. What do parents need to know to help their teens overcome the giants in their teens' lives?

3. How does the Gospel of Jesus Christ provide a road to healing and victory over the giants in our day and time?

Travis Fleming has served as the senior pastor of Union Avenue Baptist Church in Memphis, Tennessee, since September 1, 2009. He grew up in the Assemblies of God church before joining his first Southern Baptist church in 1997. He owned and operated a paint contracting company called Honest Painters, Inc. while in seminary in Louisville, Kentucky. Travis earned his BA degree in religion from North Greenville University in Tigerville, South Carolina, in 1996. He earned both his MDiv and PhD degrees from The Southern Baptist Theological Seminary in 2000 and 2006 respectively. Travis is originally from Greenville, South Carolina, and his wife Jenna is from Fort Lauderdale, Florida. They have been residents of Memphis, Tennessee, since the end of August 2009. They have two daughters, Kara and Analise. Travis is an avid fan of the Clemson Tigers.

3

ACCEPTING THE GIFT OF FRIENDSHIP

INTRODUCTION

Life is a team sport, yet far too many men today treat it as an individual one, mistakenly thinking they can live their lives without help from anyone else. They see self-sufficiency and independence as signs of strength, as much a part of manhood as having chest hair or drinking black coffee. As a result, they mask their needs behind a façade of misguided masculinity (and too much cologne). All the while, both the consistent teaching of the Bible, as well as the trying circumstances of life, keep revealing their obvious and glaring need for friendship.

This need for friendship exists even for those considered to be the manliest of men, men like David, who wrestled bears, tracked down lions, and killed a giant! In fact, the narrative of David's life is filled with situations where he was in need of help from the men around him, and there may be no situation more revealing of this truth than the one in 1 Samuel 19–20. Although David had been appointed to King Saul's service, made his armor bearer, and even welcomed into the royal family through marriage, an intense jealousy and hatred grew in Saul's heart toward David. So much so, that 1 Samuel 19 illustrates that Saul actually sought to kill David, which is why 1 Samuel 20 tells the story of David secretly reaching out to his friend Jonathan, pleading for help. So desperate was this situation that David said to Jonathan, "As surely as the LORD lives and as you yourself live, there is but a step between me and death" (1 Samuel 20:3).

David was, quite literally, at the doorstep of death, feeling its cold, foul breath breathing down his neck. While he had managed to escape Saul's first few murderous attempts, he knew there would be more, and he knew he could not run forever. Death, it seemed, was slowly closing in on him. But just as light shines brightest in the darkness, so hope is celebrated most against the backdrop of despair. And just when David seemed completely helpless and hopeless, it was then that he found hope in the help of a friend.

This story, like so many in the Bible, serves as a reminder that there is always hope with God because what His people most need, He is always faithful to provide. And what David most needed in that moment was a friend in whom he could trust, which is exactly what the Lord gave him. Jonathan was just the friend David needed for that situation, and is it not just like God to provide exactly the right friend at exactly the right time? If a bear-wrestling, lion-killing, giant-slaying specimen of a man like David still needed a friend to help him, how much more do men today need a friend like Jonathan? Thankfully, God still provides such friends. Men only need to accept the wonderful gift that God provides.

TRIALS

It is important to recognize that the desperate situation that David found himself in was not due to his disobedience to God, his lack of loyalty toward Saul, or his poor service to the king. No, just the opposite. He was at the top of Saul's "Most Wanted" list because of his God-given success: "And David had success in all his undertakings, for the LORD was with him. And when Saul saw that he had great success, he stood in fearful awe of him" (1 Samuel 18:14–15, ESV)

As men are well aware, nothing breeds jealousy quite like success. The more successful David grew, the more jealous Saul became, so much so that his jealousy grew into a murderous hatred. "Saul ordered his son Jonathan and all his servants to kill David" (1 Samuel 19:1). Twice in 1 Samuel 19, Saul tried to kill David, but twice David escaped. Fearing for his life, David then attempted to hide from Saul and his men. However, he was soon discovered. At that point, David finally came to grips with the fact that he was facing a situation he could no longer handle on his own. He was facing an enemy who was both intent on killing him and who, because he was the king, had almost everything at his disposal. Humanly speaking, David felt outmanned and outmatched.

Like David, many men today face conflicts and challenges, not because of their failure but because of their success. Others envy them because of what they have accomplished. While success usually draws attention from others, it is not always guaranteed that the attention it draws will be beneficial. Often, such attention is intended for harm; it is intended to destroy rather than to celebrate the success, like the unhealthy attention Saul paid to David. In instances such as that, men desperately need the support and assistance of a friend like Jonathan, a friend who is not threatened by, or jealous of, their success but who celebrates its God-given nature.

Therefore, while much has changed since the days of David, much has also stayed the same. It is not uncommon for men to still find themselves in situations like the one described in 1 Samuel 19–20. Granted, they may not be hunted down by a king, and they may not feel like their lives are literally threatened, but they do find themselves in situations where it seems there is no way out. They do find themselves facing circumstances they know they cannot handle on their own. They may not have had to go into hiding, but they still feel alone, isolated, and fearful. At times, they do wonder if there is anyone they can trust.

Perhaps it is a situation at work or circumstances at home where men have tried to do everything they know to do, only nothing has seemed to work. They have tried to manage the problem or crisis on their own, but now they see the futility of their own efforts. Or maybe they have tried to ignore it and pretend it will go away, but like David trying to hide from Saul, their problems keep finding them. Eventually, they realize they need help if they hope to survive the crisis. They need a friend, a friend who will be faithful and helpful in their hour of need. Like David, they desperately need God to provide a Jonathan who will stand with them and help them, which God is always faithful to do.

TRUTH

Indeed, one of the reasons that this biblical narrative proves so helpful is because it reveals both the human need *and* the divine solution. Whether men and women realize it, it is the kindness of God that reveals human need. It is His grace that leads Him to show people their inability to handle life on their own. Because then, He can also reveal that He

Himself has provided the solution to that very need. Is this not what God has done in the Gospel? He reveals the need caused by sin, but then He also shows the solution provided in Jesus Christ. He follows this same pattern for a multitude of other needs that human beings face, including the need for friendship.

So, it is important to remember that this need for friendship is a universal need that all human beings share. God did not create human beings to live in isolation and independence. He did not make people to be completely self-sufficient. Human beings are wired by their Creator for community. Even today's heavily individualistic culture seems to recognize this truth. For instance, think of the character played by Tom Hanks in the movie *Castaway.* So lonely was he on that deserted island, and so desperate was his need for friendship that he "made" a friend out of a washed-up volleyball, which he appropriately named Wilson. People readily identify with the song "Lean on Me" by Bill Withers because they know from experience that "we all need somebody to lean on." So even in a culture that highly prizes individualism and independence, it would seem that the need for friendship still exists. It is something that cannot be avoided.

The Bible clearly teaches that the reason for this universal need is that this is simply the way God created human beings. Dependence on other people is not so much a sign of weakness as it is a sign of humanity. Ecclesiastes 4:9–12 makes plain this need for others:

> Two are better than one because they have a good reward for their efforts. For if either falls, his companion can lift him up; but pity the one who falls without another to lift him up. Also, if two lie down together, they can keep warm; but how can one person alone keep warm? And if somebody overpowers one person, two can resist him.

Moreover, Proverbs 27:17 teaches that men need one another to be strengthened and sharpened: "Iron sharpens iron, and one man sharpens another." So, it is sheer folly to deny this need for friendship, when both the Bible and life itself prove it over and over again.

This should not, however, leave people feeling discouraged and hopeless because like every human need, there is a divine solution. God, in His grace, has provided for this very need. He has given humanity the gift of friendship. Therefore, it would be wise to recognize and accept the

God-given provision for this need. And again, this is where David is such a helpful model for men today.

David not only had the humility to recognize this need but also the wisdom to accept the God-given solution to it in his friend Jonathan. He refused to allow his pride to prevent him from seeing his need for help but instead sought Jonathan out and asked for his assistance. Moreover, he was willing to listen and accept Jonathan's plan of action. Such humility and wisdom is exactly what men today need to learn from David, if they hope to navigate the challenges of life that will inevitably come their way, and if they hope to benefit from the God-given gift of friendship.

So what, then, does accepting this God-given gift of friendship look like?

TRANSFORMATION

There are five lessons for men today to learn from this incident in David's life about accepting God's gracious gift of friendship. Each of them is necessary and important, and each of them needs to be put into practice if true friendship is to be honored and enjoyed. Therefore, consider these five lessons as a path that leads toward a renewed commitment of friendship or as steps on a ladder that will help you attain the joys of God's good gift of friends.

Exercising Humility

As previously implied, the first lesson to learn is the need to exercise humility. Specifically, men need to exercise humility in admitting that there are times when they need help from someone else, which, unfortunately, no man likes to do. Whether it is asking for directions, asking for a hand to lift some heavy object, or just asking for advice, men seem to have an innate stubbornness and pride that causes them to refuse to admit their need for help. But the previous sections of this chapter have sufficiently proven that regardless of a man's abilities or strength, he will face obstacles and challenges in life that he simply will not be able to handle on his own. He will need the help of a friend.

David could have stubbornly tried to handle his predicament on his own. He could have grown prideful and refused to reach out to Jonathan for help. But it would have been foolish, and probably suicidal. Instead, David exercised humility and sought out his friend: "David fled from Naioth in Ramah and *came to Jonathan* . . ." (1 Samuel 20:1, emphasis mine). The Bible says that David came looking specifically for Jonathan. David knew his need, and moreover, he knew who could help. In humility, he sought out his friend. Men today would be wise to follow the same course of action because accepting the God-given gift of friendship always begins with humbly recognizing the need for friendship.

Identifying Jonathans

Second, accepting God's gift of friendship requires men to identify the Jonathans (other faithful men) that God places around them. God will be faithful to provide men with friends, but men must be willing to see them. Men must open their eyes and look for Jonathans who demonstrate a faithful, trustworthy, and loyal spirit. They should be on the lookout for men who will be faithful friends, men they can depend on when times get tough.

There was a reason why Jonathan was the person David went looking for in 1 Samuel 20, and there was a reason why David was willing to take such a risk in reaching out to the king's son when it was the king who wanted him dead. David knew Jonathan to be faithful and loyal. He had observed these characteristics in him beforehand, and he knew that Jonathan could be counted on, even in a risky situation like this one.

Like David, men must choose their friends wisely. They must identify friends who are faithful—faithful to God, faithful to family, and faithful to others. Otherwise, the last three steps on this path will be impossible to follow. So, men need to be discerning and observing, thereby identifying the Jonathans around them that God so graciously provides.

Displaying Trust

Third, accepting God's gift of friendship requires trusting the friends that God gives. Initially, David was not sure that Jonathan was in a position to help him. He was afraid that because of their close friendship, Saul would hide his murderous plans from Jonathan, which would prevent him from being of any assistance. He even said to Jonathan, "Your father certainly knows that you have come to look favorably on me. He has said, 'Jonathan must not know of this, or else he will be grieved'" (1 Samuel 20:3). But Jonathan assured him, "Whatever you say, I will do for you" (1 Samuel 20:4).

David trusted Jonathan when he said that. He took him at his word, and they began devising a plan at that very moment. He was willing to trust that Jonathan would do whatever he could to help him out of this situation. Like David, men today have to be willing to trust their friends. They have to be willing to entrust themselves to the assistance of others, even when they are not quite sure how things will turn out. Friendship can never be enjoyed if there is not a mutual trust.

Listening to Counsel

Fourth, accepting God's gift of friendship means being willing to listen to the counsel of the friends God provides. Indeed, one of the most tangible ways for men to display the trust they have in their friends is to listen to their counsel. After David and Jonathan had developed a plan to learn of Saul's intentions, David faced another problem. He was unsure how he could be informed about whether he was finally safe or still in danger. But Jonathan offered him the following counsel:

> Tomorrow is the New Moon; you'll be missed because your seat will be empty. The following day hurry down and go to the place where you hid on the day this incident began and stay beside the rock Ezel. I will shoot three arrows beside it as if I'm aiming at a target. Then I will send the young man and say, "Go and find the arrows!" Now, if I expressly say to the young man, "Look, the arrows are on this side of you—get them," then come, because as the LORD lives, it is safe for you and there is no problem. But if I say this to the youth: "Look, the arrows are beyond you!" then go, for the LORD is sending you away (1 Samuel 20:18–22).

Jonathan counseled David to hide and wait for him to return with news of Saul's plans. Once he discerned Saul's intentions, he would come and shoot arrows and send an unknowing young man to get them, which would serve as a signal for David. Obviously, when someone's life is at stake, and he is fearful of danger lurking everywhere, simply hiding and waiting is not easy advice. But even so, David was willing to listen to Jonathan's counsel. 1 Samuel 20:24 says, "So David hid in the field." He took Jonathan's advice, as hard as it might have been. By listening to Jonathan, David was given the knowledge he needed to survive Saul's rage. Often, the hardest thing to do is also the best thing to do. Like David, men must be willing to listen to the faithful counsel of the friends God provides, even when it is hard. As Proverbs 27:9 states, "Oil and perfume make the heart glad, and the sweetness of a friend comes from his earnest counsel" (ESV).

Reciprocating Assistance

Fifth, accepting God's gift of friendship means being willing to reciprocate kindness and assistance. Friendship is a two-way street; it is both give and take. To view it otherwise is to view it selfishly. Men must be willing to give in friendship as much as they receive. David understood this aspect of friendship, and he never forgot Jonathan's assistance in this situation. 1 Samuel 20 ends with Jonathan saying to David, "Go in the assurance the two of us pledged in the name of the LORD when we said: The LORD will be a witness between you and me and between my offspring and your offspring forever" (1 Samuel 20:42).

Although that is where the chapter ends, that is not where the story ends. David continued to remember that pledge, and he eventually reciprocated the help Jonathan showed him by helping Jonathan's son, Mephibosheth, some years later. After the death of Saul and Jonathan, and the establishment of David as king, 2 Samuel 9:1 records King David asking, "Is there anyone remaining from Saul's family I can show kindness to because of Jonathan?" Once he learns about Jonathan's son, Mephibosheth, he summons him and says to him, "Don't be afraid, since I intend to show you kindness *because of your father Jonathan.* I will restore to you all your grandfather Saul's fields, and you will always eat meals at my table" (2 Samuel 9:7, emphasis mine). Jonathan's son was treated as if he were one of David's sons. Why? Because of his father and how Jonathan had helped David years earlier. David was showing kindness to Jonathan's offspring because of the kindness that Jonathan had shown him. He was reciprocating the assistance of which he himself had been the beneficiary some years prior.

If men today desire to accept and enjoy God's gift of friendship, then they must be willing not only to receive the benefits but be willing to reciprocate the kindness and assistance they themselves receive. They must be willing to give as much as they take, return the favor, and help bear someone else's burden. In other words, the last step in accepting God's gift of friendship is actually to be a friend to someone else, reciprocating the kindness that has already been experienced personally.

In God's good and wise providence, He provided a Jonathan for David. Men today must trust that He will do the same for them. They need only accept and enjoy the gift of friendship that God so faithfully provides.

QUESTIONS FOR REFLECTION

Personal Reflection

1. Do you sometimes feel like admitting that you need the help of a friend is a sign of weakness? Why do you think that is?

2. Who are some of the Jonathans in your life? As you think of them, take time right now and thank God for them.

3. Of the five steps mentioned at the end of this chapter, which one do you most need to put into practice?

4. How can you seek to be iron sharpening iron (Proverbs 27:17) for other men in your life?

Group Reflection

1. Why do men find it so hard to admit they need the help of a friend?

2. Of the five steps mentioned at the end of this chapter, is there one you think men particularly struggle to put into practice? Why or why not?

3. Practically, how can men seek to be iron sharpening iron (Proverbs 27:17) for one another?

Justin Wainscott is the pastor of First Baptist Church in Jackson, Tennessee. Justin is a graduate of Union University (BA), Beeson Divinity School (MDiv), and is currently pursuing a doctorate from The Southern Baptist Theological Seminary. He is married to Anna, and they have two children, Ella and Graham. He enjoys writing hymns and poems, and he is a lifelong Chicago Cubs fan, which has taught him much about long-suffering and perseverance.

4
RESPECTING GOD-APPOINTED LEADERS

INTRODUCTION

David is on the run. He is a wanted man. His only crime was being chosen as King Saul's successor by God Himself, but at the moment, he is not a king; he is a fugitive. As a young man, he had taken Saul's place against Goliath in the valley of Elah. Now, he had replaced Saul in the hearts of the people. They wrote songs about David. They sang his praises, and Saul intended to put an end to it. Although Saul was determined to kill the future king, David refused to harm Saul. During this time in David's life, there are two events that help one understand his view of authority. One of these times was in the wilderness of Engedi. David hid with his men in a mountain sheep fold. Pursued by King Saul and three thousand elite fighting men, David had an opportunity to kill Saul, but he refused. He had an opportunity to claim what God had already promised, but it was an opportunity to do it David's way. Another time was in the wilderness of Ziph. While Saul was sleeping, David and Abishai sneaked into his camp together. Abishai asked David to let him kill Saul with Saul's own spear. David refused because he was a man who recognized authority and that God ultimately establishes leaders.

Like David, the follower of Christ has a responsibility to respect authority and understand that God appoints leaders. The apostle Paul wrote in Romans 13.1, "Everyone must submit to the governing authorities, for there is no authority except from God; and those that exist are instituted by God." Modern society is familiar with the concept of authority and leadership. Parents, CEOs, police officers, and political figures abound. Authority definitely has its place in the world today. What does the Christian do when he works or serves under an ungodly leader? What if the issue is as simple as disagreeing with his superior? Does he have a responsibility to honor authority he does not agree with? As long as one is not asked or ordered to compromise God's Word, the answer is yes.

Believers can honor God and take great comfort by understanding that He is sovereign over the affairs of men. Christians should have two principles that guide their lives. One is to live in such a way that they honor Christ. The other is to live in such a way that they bring men to Christ. Peter understood this as he wrote in 1 Peter 2:11–17, "Dear friends, I urge you as strangers and temporary residents to abstain from fleshly desires that war against you. Conduct yourselves honorably among the Gentiles, so that in a case where they speak against you as those who do what is evil, they will, by observing your good works, glorify God on the day of visitation. Submit to every human authority because of the Lord, whether to the Emperor as the supreme authority or to governors as those sent out by him to punish those who do what is evil and to praise those who do what is good. For it is God's will that you silence the ignorance of foolish people by doing good. As God's slaves, live as free people, but don't use your freedom as a way to conceal evil. Honor everyone. Love the brotherhood. Fear God. Honor the Emperor."

TRIALS

There were times when David suffered because of his sin. But sometimes he suffered because of his faithfulness. Being faithful to God is not a guarantee that one will not experience trials. Being faithful often leads to trials in this broken world. From the moment Scripture introduces David, one sees that he is someone who respects authority. When God sent Samuel to discover the new king, David had to be called from Jesse's pasture. He was busy with the menial task of watching the sheep. The youngest of eight brothers, he probably was assigned the dirtiest and least desirable tasks among the brothers. Their estimation of him was so low that they did not even think to bring him before Samuel to be observed. One cannot know for sure if this troubled him or not, but even if it did, he was committed to the task and to authority. It is a pattern that is visible throughout his life.

What David learned as a child, he applied as a man. He learned to be faithful in the little things, which helped him be faithful in the big things. It is true that David failed miserably at times, but rather than letting that be a discouragement, it should encourage believers that even godly men have moments of failure. Luke recorded God's commendation in Acts13:22, "I have found David the son of Jesse, a man loyal to Me, who will carry out all My will." It was the disposition of David's heart that God commended, not individual actions. David's success was directly proportionate to the degree in which he was submitted to the Lord. Submission to authority (godly or otherwise) only comes when a man submits to the authority of God himself.

The modern believer faces the same challenges that David faced in his day. Of course, one need not worry about his boss throwing a spear at him or chasing him through the desert in an attempt to kill him. However, the core issues of jealousy, anger, rebellion, and ungodliness remain. Ultimately, it is pride that is at the core of every sin. Pride caused Satan's expulsion from heaven as recorded in Isaiah 14:12: "Shining morning star, how you have fallen from the heavens! You destroyer of nations, you have been cut down to the ground." Pride causes the promotion of self and leads to contention with others. It makes no difference what season of life a person is in or what vocation he pursues, the challenge of difficult people and the struggle of sin in one's own life will always be a present reality.

TRUTH

David's experience with Saul has a hint of humor to it. However, were it not for David's sense of conviction regarding Saul's divine appointment, it could have been tragic for both Saul and David. Saul went into a cave to "relieve himself," which is the biblical equivalent of saying he was completely exposed and vulnerable. David's men urged him to kill Saul, so they could all go home and resume a normal life. They were tired of being away from their families. They even tried to convince David that the Lord had given him this moment to kill Saul. David did not kill him but rather cut off a piece of his robe while Saul was preoccupied. His goal was to let Saul know that he could have killed him had he wanted. Even this simple act convicted David, and he swore he would not touch the "Lord's anointed." His respect for the Lord's authority and providence in his life kept him from sin in this instance.

David repeated this belief in the wilderness of Ziph when he had another opportunity to kill Saul. As one reads the text of 1 Samuel 26, he once again recognizes God's sovereignty over men because God allowed David and Abishai to enter Saul's camp without even being noticed—the men were in a deep sleep. Abishai changed his tactic this time and requested permission to let him kill Saul personally. "Then Abishai said to David, 'Today God has handed your enemy over to you. Let me thrust the spear through him into the ground just once. I won't have to strike him twice!'" On a personal note, Abishai's commitment and zeal for David was admirable. But once again, in verses 9–11, David repeated his conviction and rationale. "But David said to Abishai, 'Don't destroy him, for who can lift a hand against the Lord's anointed and be blameless?'" David added, "As the Lord lives, the Lord will certainly strike him down: either his day will come and he will die, or he will go into battle and perish. However, because of the Lord, I will never lift my hand against the Lord's anointed. Instead, take the spear and the water jug by his head, and let's go."

David was a warrior. He was not hesitant to take a life, but he was hesitant to violate the Lord's authority and God's Word. Similarly, the Word of God should be the source of authority in one's life. Intimacy with Christ is essential for the victorious Christian life. Paul called it keeping in step with the Spirit in Galatians 5:16–25. He lists numerous characteristics of those who are ruled by the flesh and contrasts them with the qualities of those governed by the Spirit. The key to submitting to earthly authority is found in one's submission to the authority of Christ.

A divide will always exist between worldly wisdom and biblical wisdom. Worldly counsel will always have the goal of helping one advance his personal agenda or desires. But for the believer, he has a higher agenda and a great responsibility to his Creator. Jesus told His disciples in John 15:18–19, "If the world hates you, understand that it hated Me before it hated you. If you were of the world, the world would love you as its own. However, because you are not of the world, but I have chosen you out of it, the world hates you." Followers of Christ should not expect to be loved or understood by the world. If it were true for Jesus and His disciples, should it not be true for believers today? This is not an excuse, however, for the Christian to be belligerent or contrary. Quite the opposite is true. One should treat others with reverence and respect just as Christ did and desires to do today through His people.

TRANSFORMATION

Practically, how does one bring himself to willingly submit to authority? Regardless of whether the leadership is ungodly, incompetent, or simply has a different vision for an organization, how does one respond when he finds himself in this situation? One's first inclination is generally to quit or change organizations. Even though sometimes that is possible, it is not always right. Here is the crisis of the heart. The Christian must first ask himself the questions: How does God want to change me through this situation? What does God want to accomplish through this situation? How does God want to change this situation? Exploratory questions like these help one reframe the situation from a worldly, personal perspective to a kingdom perspective. For this writer, the realization that he is only a part of God's kingdom and not the center of it should provide tremendous comfort. David did not choose to retaliate against Saul because he knew that ultimately God was in control. How did he have the confidence that God was with him when he faced Goliath? Because he knew God was with him when he killed a lion and a bear. How could he respect Saul's position without agreeing with Saul? The answer is simple: because he trusted and followed God.

If understanding that God has a purpose for every situation brings clarity, the next step brings power. Respecting authority is not natural because of one's sin nature. From an early age, we are taught to respect authority because it is socially acceptable. Because that is what good children do. But there is nothing more frustrating than trying to perform a spiritual act in the power of the flesh. If rebellion began in the Garden of Eden, submission for the Christian begins at the cross. The apostle Paul wrote in Philippians 2:5–8, "Make your own attitude that of Christ Jesus, who, existing in the form of God, did not consider equality with God as something to be used for His own advantage. Instead He emptied Himself by assuming the form of a slave, taking on the likeness of men. And when He had come as a man in His external form, He humbled Himself by becoming obedient to the point of death—even to death on a cross." Submission to Christ is the key. When one gives his life to Christ, Jesus gives His life in return, and everything that Jesus did becomes accessible and expressed in the life of the believer. By giving us His nature, Jesus did not only make us fit for heaven, but He also made us fit to live on earth. The victory won by Christ at the cross is a pervasive victory for those who come in faith to Christ. It is Christ living His life in and through believers that provides the power to accomplish His purpose. If "Christ in us" does not live "His life" through us, then the ability to walk in power and fruitfulness will be depleted if we depend on our own strength (Galatians 2:20). All believers must yield in submission to God's rule in every area of life. Paul wrote in 1 Corinthians 6:19–20, "Don't you know that your body is a sanctuary of the Holy Spirit who is in you, whom you have from God? You are not your own, for you were bought at a price. Therefore glorify God in your body."

Understand what God is trying to accomplish, submit to His authority, rely upon His power, and leave the results to Him. As Paul stated in Ephesians 3:20–21, "Now to Him who is able to do above and beyond all that we ask or think according to the power that works in us—to Him be glory in the church and in Christ Jesus to all generations, forever and ever. Amen."

Scripture provides details about decades of David's life. Certainly, as a "man after God's own heart" (Acts 13:22), David provided many examples of faithfulness. His respect for authority is one of those areas of faithfulness. Had David not responded to those in authority over him in a way that reflected his deep love for God and respect for His Word, Saul's life would have likely ended prematurely. David suffered because of his committed respect. God used those times of suffering to shape his heart and life in preparation for him to be king.

It is very difficult to evaluate the long-term sovereignty of God and His ability to march His plans out over time when we view it in individual, short-term moments. It is often easy for any believer to feel that a leader, who is in authority over them, is neither leading effectively nor faithfully. Our response should be a biblically shaped response that reflects both the heart and will of God. The Spirit of God gives believers the ability to make faithful, God-honoring choices even when it appears that a fleshly response is justified. It is the Spirit of God that enabled David to remain faithful when he and his friends wanted to respond differently (1 Samuel 16:13). It is the Spirit of God that enables us to reflect God's character and His Word when confronting someone in authority who appears to be less than faithful with the platform of influence they occupy. God is good and faithful! He can even use unfaithful people in positions of authority to shape the hearts of His people to be more like Him.

QUESTIONS FOR REFLECTION

Personal Reflection

1. Am I willing to submit to the leaders God has placed over me? Why or why not?

2. What steps do I need to take to change my attitude concerning submission to authority?

3. Is there any area of my life I have not surrendered to the Lordship of Christ?

4. How can I invest in others and teach them how to submit to Christ?

Group Reflection

1. How did David's relationship with the Lord affect his relationship with others?

2. Does a believer have to agree with someone to respect him? Do we respect the person or the position of authority?

3. How can respecting those in authority be a witness for Christ?

Cliff Pace is the senior pastor of Hernando Baptist in northwest Mississippi, a thriving congregation in one America's fastest growing counties. Their aim is to communicate the gospel through truth and transformed lives. Cliff holds a master of divinity from New Orleans Baptist Theological Seminary and is currently a doctoral student at Southwestern Baptist Theological Seminary. Cliff and his wife, Tracy, reside in Hernando, Mississippi. They have two girls, Shaohannah Jane and Sadie Caroline, and are expecting their third child in March, as well as pursuing their second adoption from China. He enjoys participating in any sport, except basketball, and is an avid runner and cyclist in his spare time.

5

PURSUING THE PRESENCE OF GOD

INTRODUCTION

David is one of the Bible's larger-than-life heroes. He was the original warrior-poet, ruler of Israel's golden age, and lead worshipper of the one true God. Because of his exciting life, many Bible readers look at his life as one victory after another. To men, David seems too good to be true. These readers do not realize that David's life was one of success and failure, marked by repentance and a desire to honor the Lord.

David's Desire for God's Presence

Second Samuel 6 describes David's pursuit of the presence of God. Having captured Jerusalem, David prepared to bring the Ark of the Covenant into the city. The ark was the physical reminder of God's presence with them, His earthly footstool and symbolic dwelling place.[1] Having the ark in Jerusalem would be a spiritual and political victory for David: the Lord would have a permanent place of worship, and His presence would signify His blessing on Israel's new king.[2]

David gathered an army of his best men to accompany the ark into the city. He desired to please the Lord so much that he had his men

---

[1] Eugene H. Peterson, First and Second Samuel, (Louisville: Westminster John Knox, 1999), 161.

[2] Joyce G. Baldwin, 1 & 2 Samuel, (Downers Grove: Inter Varsity Press, 1988), 205.

make a new cart, undefiled and clean, to carry the ark from Baale-judah into Jerusalem. David danced before the Lord, celebrating God's presence and blessing in his life. As the oxen pulled the ark in the new cart, they stumbled. Without thinking, one of the men accompanying the sacred box reached out his hand to steady it. Having profaned the ark, God struck him dead.

David reacted to this judgment with anger, perhaps, caused by fear and embarrassment. He gave up his pursuit, returned the ark to a countryman's house, and went back to Jerusalem. Three months later, having been reminded of the blessing of God's presence, David returned for the ark. He replicated his first attempt, only this time he insured that the ark was transported according to God's instruction. During this move, David experienced true worship, learned about God's holiness, dealt with his own emotions, and in the end, enjoyed the blessing of God's presence in his life.

Desiring God's Presence Today

David's life does not serve as a goal for today's men; they certainly do not need to be like David! However, many of the same challenges and desires that David faced in his relationship with the Lord and the world so long ago are similar to many contemporary challenges. Christian men struggle with excelling in the public world, while attempting to live for Christ. They are tempted to quit pursuing worship when they are embarrassed by mistakes, are ashamed of their emotions, or when they feel that God expects too much from them. The fear of failure, shame, and/or even judgment prompts men, too often, to slink into the shadows of church, settling for the edges rather than the center of the Lord's presence.

With the Lord, however, there is hope! God desires to be with His people. His eternal plan for those who belong to Him is conformity to the image of Christ. As He did with David, God will use events in His followers' lives to shape them into men after His own heart.

TRIALS

Simply making it in the twenty-first century is a difficult endeavor. Men combat the desire to run away from jobs, debt, family, and even God. To attempt the pursuit of God's presence may not be on the radar of most men. For many, they have done their best by showing up at church once a week! David shared the same trials while seeking God. He struggled with direction, discouragement, and desire as he worshipped God.

When Devotion Overlooks Direction

Because of David's history with God, his heart was already settled in devotion to God. Such devotion caused him to gather "all the choice men in Israel, 30,000" (2 Samuel 6:1). This select army represented the best David and Israel had to offer, as well as representing those who were killed in battle when the ark was taken from them.[3] It was his sense of honor that led him to transport the ark in "a new cart . . . from Abinidab's house" (6:3). "David and the whole house of Israel" (6:5) celebrated before the Lord, an expression of his great love for his God.

In the excitement of the moment, however, David overlooked God's instructions on how He was to be worshipped. David's new cart was not God's plan for transporting the ark. David disregarded God's directions in his approach to worship, and as "the oxen stumbled" (6:6), the unthinkable happened. Uzzah touched the symbol of God's presence to steady it from falling. Immediately, "God struck him dead on the spot for his irreverence" (6:7).

Like David, men today bear many responsibilities. A man loves his wife, leads his children, and serves at church, all from a sense of devotion to his family and the Lord. Even with the best intentions, attempting to fulfill those God-given ministries without biblical instruction will result in failure. When devotion overlooks God's direction, frustration and difficulty often follow.

---

[3] Kenneth Chafin, 1, 2 Samuel, (Dallas: Word Publishing, 1989), 274-5.

When Discipline Brings Discouragement

God's discipline for Uzzah's irreverence and David's error was immediate. Uzzah's death angered the king (6:8). The Bible does not explain why David was angry. Perhaps his anger burned because he knew that he was responsible for the situation. Maybe he thought God should have been more patient toward Uzzah. Whatever the cause, he got mad at God.

As a worshipper, David feared the presence of God (6:9). His experience with returning the ark led him to believe that God's presence was no longer an exciting place of dancing and celebration. God's judgment against sin frightened David. As the worship leader, he was embarrassed before his people. How could God expect him to lead after this obvious failure?

When I was twenty-three years old, I was stationed in Germany while in the army. Married that May, it was six months before my wife came to live with me. Our first real outing together as newlyweds came on Thanksgiving, two weeks after my bride arrived. Being a habitual tease, I made a joke at my wife's expense during dinner. My heart was right—I didn't mean anything by it—so how could it hurt?

The host of the home, a missionary to soldiers there, spoke discipline into my life. "Jim," he said softly, "we don't make jokes at our wives' expense." I was one of the leaders of the ministry, and his words stung. As an adult, I had never been called down in public. He was right, but it took effort for me to understand that. I struggled with anger and embarrassment.

Many men, desiring to honor the Lord and be devoted to their wives and families, find themselves in the same place as David. It becomes easy at times to approach God with the motto: it's the thought that counts. God, however, calls His children to faithful obedience. When they fall short, He "disciplines the one He loves" (Hebrews 12:6). This discipline, delivered by a loving heavenly Father, can bring discouragement to those who are unprepared to receive it.

When Defeat Smothers Desire

David reacted to God's response as most men would. He quit. The sting of discipline coupled with the perceived loss of face caused him to pack up his things and go home. The Bible says that he "was not willing to move the ark" so he took it to the house of Obed-edom instead (2 Samuel 6:10).

It remains important to understand the implications of David's decision to quit. In his day, the Ark of the Covenant was the greatest picture of the Lord's presence with His people. Everywhere the ark went, God's power was manifest and blessings followed. David allowed his emotions to rob him of intimacy with God, stripping him of the opportunity to see God's power and blessing. His discouragement led to his own defeat.

Today's churches are filled with men who once had a white-hot passion for the Lord. For one reason or another, they viewed God's instruction and discipline as too great a burden to bear. Those men now sit on the sidelines, either afraid of God or angry toward Him. They do not know the intimacy of God's presence because they have shied away from Him. They are discouraged and disengaged. They have forfeited the opportunity to know God's power and blessing.

TRUTH

The possibility remains that, having heard of God's judgment against Uzzah and His discipline toward David, men may think it is safer to stay away from God than to risk His presence. David thought that very thing. He had experienced incomparable fulfillment in his life with God; he then discovered the great loss of intimacy without the presence of God.

Recognizing the Loss of God's Presence

The Bible seems to indicate that even while the ark rested in Obed-edom's home, David continued to long for it (1 Chronicles 15:1). In the interim, he built a tent to house the ark of the Lord. The ark stayed with Obed-edom for three months (2 Samuel 6:11), while David began his reign from the city of Jerusalem. But all the while, David seemed to have kept an eye on the ark to see if judgment or blessing would come to the house of Obed-edom.

The reason David felt such a sense of loss had nothing to do with the outward rituals of his religion. David desired his relationship with God to be restored. From his boyhood, his life was marked by God's presence. He knew the Lord, followed the Lord, and loved the Lord. For the ark, the one indicator of God's presence with His people, to be outside of God's city was a constant reminder of the separation that sin brings.

Mankind was created to enjoy fellowship with God. The Lord God made a special home for Adam (Genesis 2:8). Adam was given fulfilling work to do by his Creator (Genesis 2:15). Scripture indicates that God spent time regularly with Adam and Eve (Genesis 3:8).[4] Once Adam disobeyed God, man recognized the separation that sin brought. No longer enjoying God's presence, Adam hid from God. Apart from God's presence, he felt guilty, ashamed, and afraid. Humans today are the recipients of both legacies: we recognize a yearning for something more—divine intimacy—but our sinful choices result instead in guilt, shame, and fear before God.

Today, those who experience the reconciliation to our heavenly Father available through Christ know the loss when sin strains the relationship once more. To have lived in the fullness of the Holy Spirit and then have to settle for the best flesh can do brings a huge void in one's life. Some men today, seated in our Sunday school classes and comfortable in our pews, navigate through this life with a critical lack of spiritual vitality. Once surrendered to the Holy Spirit and enjoying God's presence in their lives, they now struggle through each day, sensing the loss even without knowing the cause.

Realizing the Blessing of God's Presence

David was not the only one keeping an eye on Obed-edom's home. Others were watching to see if God's presence was a blessing or a curse to him. Those watching "reported to King David: 'The Lord has blessed Obed-edom's family and all that belongs to him because of the ark of God'" (2 Samuel 6:12a).

---

[4] Literally "the breezy time of the day," but could be rendered "the spiritual time of the day."

Fear had gripped the king, so he distanced himself from the symbol of the presence of God. But that fear was overcome by joy when he realized that God's presence to those in relationship with Him was a blessing, not a curse. "So David went and had the ark of God brought up from Obed-edom's house to the city of David with rejoicing" (2 Samuel 6:12b).

From the moment humankind sinned and was separated from God, God began seeking to restore the relationship. Restoration has always been God's intention (Acts 3:19–21). That search culminated in the person of Jesus the Messiah. Prophesying of His arrival, Isaiah said, "And they will name him Immanuel, which is translated 'God is with us'" (Matthew 1:23). God is with us! In Jesus, the Father revealed the promise of His presence. All that was broken by sin can be restored in Jesus.

Great hope exists for men who have stumbled over failure or been stung by rebuke. God promises His presence, and that presence is a great blessing and a joy. Nothing short of God's presence, however, satisfies our purpose for being. The average American man looks to possessions, promotions, or pursuits to satisfy that purpose. These substitutes distract men and keep them from true worship. As one looks around the fellowship at church and sees joyful men, their secret does not rest in the successes of this world but in the blessings of God's presence.

Receiving the Benefit of God's Presence

Because of the report of those watching, and the apparent blessings on Obed-edom's household, David decided to retrieve the ark once more. This time, David moved it in a way that pleased the Lord. First, he had it carried, as God had instructed for it to be moved (2 Samuel 6:13). Second, he "sacrificed an ox and a fattened calf" to the Lord that demonstrated his whole-hearted worship (6:13). These outward activities demonstrated an inward desire to honor God. David wanted to be right with God and longed for a restored relationship.

God blessed David's desire for restoration. The Lord allowed the ark to be brought into Jerusalem without further judgment. God's symbolic presence now rested in the City of David. This experience caused David to be filled with joy. He demonstrated that joy as he led out in worship, leaping and dancing with shouts of triumph. David was restored to the Lord as friend, worshipper, and king. Even his wife's ridicule did not dim his joy. David was fulfilled because he was right with God (2 Samuel 6:20–22).

Men need not seek the ark of God today as a symbol of His presence. For those in a relationship with Him through Jesus, He has given us the permanence of His presence. God has given Himself, through the person of the Holy Spirit, to live within and lead His people. The Holy Spirit empowers the believer to worship and serve God rightly, and guarantees God's presence always. The joy of blessing that David experienced is the birthright of every Christ follower.

This truth may seem like a dry, Sunday school doctrine to those who hear without personal experience. Instead, this reality is the ultimate blessing. God is with us! Regardless of the situation or problem, men never have to experience separation from God again, once they put their trust in Jesus. If a man belongs to Christ and is surrendered to His Spirit, he will enjoy the blessing of the presence of God: the purpose of man's existence fulfilled! In the sixteenth psalm, David said it best, "In Your presence is abundant joy" (Psalms 16:11).

TRANSFORMATION

Twin dangers exist as men seek to fulfill their God-given roles in the world. First, men are tempted to compartmentalize their relationship with God. They may think that walking with God is a "Sunday thing," separated from the "real world." This could not be further from the truth. The men of the Bible were publicly marked by the presence of God on their lives. The quest for a fulfilled life must begin in the presence of God.

Second, men may be tempted to pursue a relationship with God through mere religious activities. It can be easy to read the account of David retrieving the ark as an extension of his religious duty. Read this way, David retrieved, sacrificed, and danced because he was trying to earn merit with God. This approach, however, misses the reality of experiencing God. These activities do not earn God's presence but are responses to His presence.

So, how should a man respond to the scriptural example that David set as he sought God's presence? Apart from the presence of God in man's life, there can be no lasting transformation; no sure focus for the future; and, ultimately, no real joy. It is just that simple.

Establishing the Relationship

The transformation of our hearts begins with a relationship with God, which is initiated by His gracious pursuit of us. God created men and women to enjoy a relationship with Him, but as already noted, man's sin against God brought separation. At this point, many men look for something they must do to overcome that separation. They may ask, "Is there an ark around I can go get?" or "Is there a quest I can pursue to find God?" Mankind's first reaction to separation is to overcome it through action.

The problem with the separation caused by sin is that man cannot overcome it on his own. No amount of good deeds or adventuresome quests can account for sin. The good news about this separation is that God has acted to bridge the gap. Immanuel, which means, "God is with us," is also called Jesus, "because He will save His people from their sins" (Matthew 1:21). Jesus lived a perfect life, died on the cross for our sins according to Scripture, and rose again from the dead to live forever. He acted to restore sinners to God.

For sinners to be restored, however, they must respond to Jesus' activity. A sinner must recognize that his sin is against God. He must turn from that sin, placing his faith in Jesus' finished work on the cross as the only foundation for his relationship with God. The Bible says, "If you confess with your mouth, 'Jesus is Lord,' and believe in your heart that God raised Him from the dead, you will be saved" (Romans 10:9).

Some Christians think that this Gospel only gains us entrance into heaven. On the contrary, this Gospel secures eternal life in heaven but also promises fulfillment here on earth (John 5:24). The presence of God David enjoyed, and danced over, is available to all who seek Him and realize the need for a Savior. This relationship must be established before one can know God's presence.

Enjoying the Relationship

Having been introduced by faith in Jesus into this relationship, men can begin to actually enjoy God. His presence is the mark of His blessing, and it really is His greatest gift to man. This gift can be enjoyed more fully as it is explored and cherished.

All that men know about this blessing is found in Scripture. God's Word reveals His character, interprets man's experiences, and grows them in wisdom and knowledge of Him. In order to know how to relate to God, men must give themselves to His Word. Because of this, the first step in enjoying God's presence is the delving into Scripture and allowing God's very words to reshape our perspective, our desires, and how we spend our money and time.

Men tend to be hesitant when it comes to reading anything, especially the Bible. At times, Scripture seems to be mysterious, as if one cannot know what he should glean from it. However, it helps to have an aim in mind when reading. For the purpose of seeking the presence of God, one can read, seeking to know more about Him. This approach explores His words (what He said), His works (what He did), and His ways (how He works) throughout Scripture. As these are identified, one begins to see God's activity in one's own life.

The relationship that embraces God's presence in a believer's life is revealed in Scripture but strengthened through prayer. Christians are accustomed to public prayer during worship times and before meals, but often struggle with a consistent, private prayer life. It is in prayer, though, that men interact with the living God. As man speaks with God, he develops the relationship that promises God's presence. Prayer invites God's power into daily situations, allowing the community to see God and giving God glory through a person's life.

Perhaps the most confusing of all practices is the practice of public worship. In the account of David's leadership found in 2 Samuel 6, all that he did could be defined as public worship. He sacrificed, prayed, danced, marched, and shouted in worship of the Lord. Rarely do men have the opportunity to exercise in worship in quite the same way. It would be quite the sight for an usher to dance his way down the center aisle during the giving of the tithes and offerings!

That kind of enthusiastic heart is necessary for meaningful worship. It is not necessarily the outward expression that matters. What counts is the heart that offers the activity. Too often, men are detached and unengaged in public worship, choosing to check texts or read the bulletin, so they never prepare their own hearts for public worship. When this happens, they do not truly worship and never experience the joy of God's presence in public worship.

Those who do prepare their hearts for worship enjoy God's tangible presence. In those moments, God gives peace and purpose to those who seek after Him. Church services come alive as worshippers are engaged by the Object of their worship. No substitute exists for meaningful public worship.

Employing the Relationship

When a man has a relationship with God through Jesus and learns to enjoy the presence of God that accompanies it, the results affect every area of his life. No area remains untouched as God transforms His man. God's presence in a man's life indelibly marks him, and that mark spills out into all of his earthly relationships.

Because of the proximity, this transformation can be seen most readily by his family. In several places in the New Testament, Scripture instructs husbands in the way to interact with their wives.[5] These instructions emerge from discussions regarding the marks of the Spirit-led conduct of a believer. The presence of God influences a man's behavior toward his wife, but also toward his children. He can now lead them in worship and in pursuit of their own relationships with God.

God's presence also affects a man as he relates to the community of worshippers. This occasion, known as "going to church," is really much bigger than we imagine. Public worship should be the greatest display of God's presence on the earth. Men, who are filled with God's presence, gathering together with unity of purpose, are not content to settle for the mundane or mediocre. They seek the Lord, are directed by Him, and enjoy the various ways He is glorified through the worship service. As this happens, a church's worship gatherings become far from boring.

Finally, a man marked by the Lord's presence stands out in his community. Because of the holiness of God's presence, as men surrender

---

[5] See Ephesians 5 and 1 Peter 3.

to His leadership they, too, will be marked by holiness. A man's first response to this notion might be to shrink back and say, "I can't be holy." The beauty of God's presence is that He accomplishes that work of holiness in a surrendered life. Man surrenders to God, and God does the work.

Not only is a believing man marked by God's holiness, he is also be marked by God's power. God's presence causes demons to tremble, kings to bow, and idols to fall. That power, filling an individual, has the potential to overwhelm a neighborhood, school, or jobsite with the grace of God. Perhaps the only way to see a nation change its course would be the power of the presence of God displayed through men surrendered to Him.

Many men read of the exploits of King David and wonder what it would be like to be so successful, so powerful. Too often, those readers ascribe his success to the things he did, rather than the One whom he pursued. David's "secret" to success was a heart that was tender toward God and a life marked by His presence. Today's Christian man can enjoy the same type of experiences—those that accompany the presence of God.

QUESTIONS FOR REFLECTION

Personal Reflection

1. Would you classify your spiritual life as one marked by the presence of God? Why or why not?

2. Can you identify the last time you experienced God's presence? If you are not experiencing that intimate presence today, what happened?

3. If you said that your life is marked by God's presence, how does it affect your home, church, and community life? If not, what would you like God to change in those areas?

Group Reflection

1. Have you ever witnessed a moment of failure like the one recorded in 2 Samuel 6:1–11? How did that affect your desire to worship?

2. How would you characterize David's repentance here?

3. How difficult is it for you to distinguish between outward (religious) acts of worship and inward (relational) worship?

4. What do you do to stay focused on your relationship?

5. How can you as a group transform public worship within your church?

6. Can you identify a time when God disciplined you? How did you react? (Hebrews 12:5–6).

Jim Collier is the pastor of Kirby Woods Baptist Church in Memphis, Tennessee, serving there since October 2008. He is currently a doctoral candidate at Mid-America Baptist Theological Seminary, hoping to graduate in December 2014. He is a product of God's smiling providence in the form of loving Christian parents, the US Army Ranger School, and a Carolina girl who said, "I do." Jim and Myra have been married for twenty years. They have two wonderful children, Rebecca and Joshua. Before answering God's call to preach, Jim served in the United States Army for twelve years, in both the enlisted and officer ranks.

6
THE CONSEQUENCES OF IGNORING GOD'S PURPOSE

INTRODUCTION

Give this question some thought: What is God's purpose for your life? Be careful, because it is so easy to slip into a self-centered mode rather than a Christ-centered mode as you contemplate your answer. Here is a personal story that might shed some light on this issue.

Twenty-nine years ago, I learned a valuable lesson relating to God's purpose. In 1976, I graduated from Mississippi State University with a degree in education. As a follower of Christ, I was certain that coaching and teaching was God's purpose for my life. For eight years, I poured my life into students and their parents, and I did so with an unashamed desire to please the Lord. My wife loved being a coach's wife. For this season, needless to say, everything seemed to be set.

When 1983 rolled around, the Lord Jesus began to open doors for me to speak in our church and then in nearby churches. Strangely, a desire to preach the Word began to grow, and my life-long desire to coach and teach began to diminish. This turn of events culminated in a sweaty locker room the summer prior to a new season.

The locker room, abounding with its distinct odor and a host of memories, became my early morning sanctuary that summer. I was painting the walls and building new lockers. The radio was turned to a Christian station that offered solid Bible teaching every morning. My heart's desire was to obey God, but I was confused about my future. Did my Lord want me to coach and teach or to preach the Word?

John MacArthur's sermon that morning focused on 1 Timothy 3:1—"This saying is trustworthy: 'If anyone aspires to be an overseer, he desires a noble work.'" He explained that God often reveals His will through the desires He places in our hearts. Believe me; I knew that a passion to preach the Word had gripped my heart like a vice-grip. That old, sweaty locker room became holy ground as I fell to my knees and poured out my heart to the Lord in full surrender to His *new* purpose for my life.

Let's be clear here. Jesus has every right to do whatever He wants to do with your life. He said, ". . . If anyone wants to come with Me, he must deny himself, take up his cross daily, and follow Me" (Luke 9:23). By His grace, you are saved from your sins and you have become a part of His eternal family. As the Gospel is worked out in your life, you begin to be conformed to the image of Jesus, actively involved in serving Him and advancing His eternal kingdom. He has the power to leverage your business savvy, your engineering know-how, your mechanical ability, or your love of nurturing your family for His glory and the advancement of His kingdom.

Are you living in the sweet spot of God's purpose for your life? He is gracious and patient with us as He shapes us and nudges us. Nevertheless, ignoring God's purpose for your life can be painful and even shameful. David is a perfect example of this truth.

The story of David's life is amazing to say the least. He had a heart for the Lord from an early age. God selected David to be the king of Israel. His mission was to lead God's covenant people with integrity and passion for the Lord. Unfortunately, David made two decisions that defied God's purpose for his life, and both of these resulted in devastating circumstances.

David was around fifty years old when he stepped on a moral landmine during a time of great vulnerability. The Bible lays out the scene for us: "In the spring when kings march out to war, David sent Joab with his officers and all Israel. They destroyed the Ammonites and besieged Rabbah, but David remained in Jerusalem" (2 Samuel 11:1).

Do not miss the significance of this verse. David should have been with his army fighting the Lord's battles, but he stayed behind. Chuck Swindoll remarked, "Had he been where he belonged—with his troops—there would never have been the Bathsheba episode. Our greatest battles don't usually come when we're working hard; they come when we have some leisure, when we've got time on our hands, when we're bored."[1] A failure to fulfill God's purpose in this situation resulted in an adulterous encounter with Bathsheba and the eventual murder of her husband, Uriah the Hittite.

Near the end of David's reign, he blatantly disregarded God's purpose for his life a second time. Under the king's leadership, Israel was experiencing a time of peace and success. Pride reared its ugly head, and David ordered Joab to conduct a census so he could celebrate his accomplishments. God's glory was not even a blip on David's radar screen. This foolish decision impacted thousands of lives.

One thing about David stands out. He took responsibility for his rash decisions and their fallout. In each case, he repented of his sin and cried out to God for forgiveness. God, in turn, forgave him and restored him.

As you dive into this chapter, you might be hammering yourself because of some poor decisions you made that swept you right out of God's purpose for your life. Do not give up on yourself. The same God who forgave and restored David can forgive and restore you.

TRIALS

God takes sin seriously, and the consequences of sin have a ripple effect. The list of men who believe otherwise is endless. Here is a scenario that is all too common. A man comes into his pastor's office and offers this bit of theological insight: "Pastor, I know that God wants the best for me. Recently I met a woman whom I truly believe is my soul mate. She makes me happy, happy, happy (a little *Duck Dynasty* thrown in). Therefore, I am asking my wife for a divorce. It is not healthy for the kids to live in a home where their dad is not in love with their mom."

Lean forward to give your full attention to this statement. No one will find happiness and fulfillment by turning his nose up at the purpose of God for his life. God's will is for a man to stay married within the confines of his covenant relationship. No new desire will nullify what God has already declared to be His will. This is just as true for us as it was true for David.

---

[1] Charles R. Swindoll, A Man of Passion & Destiny, David, (Dallas: Word Publishing, 1997) 183.

David's Attempt to Cover Up His Sin

David was a brilliant and bold warrior as well as a wise and engaging king. If anybody could handle a moral meltdown, surely he could. Sure enough, he schemed and strategized in an effort to cover his devious tracks. Despite his best efforts, one thing after another unraveled like a worn-out shirt.

Bathsheba was pregnant. Uriah was David's committed soldier and Bathsheba's loyal husband. What a tangled web! David, in an effort to cover up his sin, sent for Uriah and brought him home. In spite of David's best efforts to induce him to sleep with Bathsheba, he refused to do so because of his loyalty to his troops. The king's immorality was squarely in the spotlight now. What would he do?

A thought crept into David's mind that must have shocked even him. God's Word reveals his dreadful intention—"The next morning David wrote a letter to Joab and sent it with Uriah. In the letter he wrote: Put Uriah at the front of the fiercest fighting, then withdraw from him so that he is struck down and dies" (2 Samuel 11:14–15). Adultery, and now murder, ripped away at the moral fabric of David's life. Can you imagine what it must have been like for him as he sought to conceal his sin? Three chilling words define the root cause of David's actions. David forgot God!

He had obviously forgotten that God had chosen him to be Israel's king because of his spiritual integrity. He forgot that God had given him great victories that in turn had made him famous. All the abundant blessings that God had poured out in his lap were forgotten. Evidently, he thought he had beaten the system. That is until Nathan, the prophet, showed up.

God sent Nathan to confront David, and confront him he did. The scene is depicted for us in the Bible:

> Nathan replied to David, "You are the man! This is what the Lord God of Israel says: 'I anointed you king over Israel, and I delivered you from the hand of Saul. I gave your master's house to you and your master's wives into your arms, and I gave you the house of Israel and Judah, and if that was not enough, I would have given you even more. Why then have you despised the command of the Lord by doing what I consider evil? You struck down Uriah the Hittite with the sword and took his wife as your

> own wife—you murdered him with the Ammonite's sword. . . . (2 Samuel 12:7–9).

David learned a valuable lesson that day. You cannot conceal your sin from God!

The Impact of David's Sin on His Family

Can you imagine how David's heart must have been broken as he was forced to face God's discipline? Like a ricocheting bullet, the people he loved the most were affected. He and Bathsheba's love child died. He witnessed the disintegration of his children through blatant immorality, murder, insurrection, and a lack of respect for their dad. Furthermore, he lost the moral high ground that every leader needs in order to be successful. He literally had to run for his own life because his son led a coup against him and was trying to kill him. What a price to pay for a few moments of forbidden passion!

The Impact of David's Sin on the Nation

David repented of his sin and God restored him to lead Israel. He was blessed to see God pour out His favor on the nation once again. Unfortunately, the king became somewhat proud of his own achievements and wanted to measure his own success. When he ordered a census, it did not take him long to discover that God was highly displeased with his self-centered actions. The Bible records these words: "This command was also evil in God's sight, so He afflicted Israel" (1 Chronicles 21:7).

God afflicted Israel. Seventy-thousand Jewish men died as a result of David's blatant disregard for God's purpose and God's glory. Can you imagine how he must have felt? The Bible reveals this interesting insight through David's own words—". . . I have great anxiety" (2 Samuel 24:14). These words mean, "to be tied up, restricted, cramped."[2] He was miserable!

---

[2] Swindoll, 277.

Facing Our Own Trials

How many men do you know who have blown it morally and are facing trials of their own? Take a long, hard look at the collateral damage that has been inflicted upon their wives and children. Do not think for a moment that you are an exception to the case. Pride like David displayed can seep into your life and bring you down also.

Every man alive today has to deal with our sex-crazed culture, which is brimming over with pornography, revealing clothes, and a total disregard for moral standards. Satan's goal is to wear us down, to numb us spiritually, and to wreak havoc in our lives and in the lives of those we love. Men, whatever you do, count the cost! If you are being squeezed by Satan's temptation at this moment, think about the effect your failure will have upon your Lord's reputation, your family, your church, your finances, your health, your integrity, and your career. Stop fantasizing and get real!

Have you already had a moral and spiritual collapse? One truth that surfaces when you study the life of David is this: failure does not have to be final! God is gracious and forgiving if we truly repent and seek Him with all our hearts. I wish I could tell you that He will undo all the painful consequences. He will not do that. You, like David, must absorb those blows without blaming God. You must take full responsibility for your actions, and you must trust the Lord to heal the hurts of those who have been impacted by your sinful decision. Know this: your life can still count for God!

TRUTH

A Jewish proverb says this—*Truth is heavy, so few men carry it.* There is a lot of truth to that statement (no pun intended). David became oblivious to God's Word as he blindly walked down a road of disobedience. Truth, that God intended for protection and blessing, was ignored and David paid the price. Let us look at a few truths that David disregarded.

The Relevance of God's Word

David's life was slowly coming apart before his night of enchantment with Bathsheba. The Word says, "Then David knew that the Lord had established him as king over Israel and had exalted his kingdom for the sake of His people Israel. After he arrived from Hebron, David took more concubines and wives from Jerusalem, and more sons and daughters were born to him" (2 Samuel 5:12–13). Multiplying one's wives and children was normal for kings in David's day. There's only one problem with that. God expressly prohibited this practice for Jewish kings—"He must not acquire many wives for himself so that his heart won't go astray. He must not acquire very large amounts of silver and gold for himself" (Deuteronomy 17:17).

How could David miss something that was so plain? He had a harem of wives and concubines, but he still committed adultery with Bathsheba and had her husband killed. He was blinded by his own prideful and lustful heart.

Being a Jew meant that he had a deep love and appreciation for the Jewish Law. The seventh commandment says, "Do not commit adultery" (Exodus 20:14). The tenth one says, "Do not covet your neighbor's house. Do not covet your neighbor's wife, his male or female slave, his ox or donkey, or anything that belongs to your neighbor" (Exodus 20:17). David ran through every red light that God erected in front of him and, as a result, wrecked his life and the lives of others.

The Need for God's Word

Here's another truth that would have saved David a lot of humiliation, tears, and grief. Again, Moses recorded a portion of God's Word that was specifically dedicated to the future kings of Israel. He wrote, "When he is seated on his royal throne, he is to write a copy of this instruction for himself on a scroll in the presence of the Levitical priests. It is to remain with him, and he is to read from it all the days of his life, so that he may learn to fear the Lord his God, to observe all the words of this instruction, and to do these statutes. Then his heart will not be exalted above his countrymen, he will not turn from this command to the right or the left, and he and his sons will continue ruling many years over Israel" (Deuteronomy 17:18–20). The king had access to the first five books of the Bible, and he had the resources to produce his own personal copy. Had he studied the Word and allowed it to permeate his mind and heart, the moral meltdown with Bathsheba and the foolish decision to conduct a census could have been avoided.

God's Awareness of Sin

Make no mistake about it; David was a man after God's own heart, but he fell hard for the enemy's temptation, and one sin built upon another until his heart was hardened to the things of God. Can you believe that this man's mind was so clouded that he actually thought he could hide his sin from God? Surely he had read the book of Genesis where God's Word to Cain was certainly an eye-opener. God said to him, "If you do what is right, won't you be accepted? But if you do not do what is right, sin is crouching at the door. Its desire is for you, but you must rule over it" (Genesis 4:7). The living God knew exactly what Cain was cooking up in his heart (the murder of his brother), and He warned him to back off. Again, God's truth sailed right over David's head without making an impact.

The Truth for Today

This list of truths that David obviously ignored is not exhaustive. Each of these truths was available in the Word of God that David had access to at the time. The point is clear. Every man needs to orient his life around God's Word. This is called a biblical worldview. Josh and Sean McDowell wrote:

> The Christian faith was then and still is an integrated and organic cycle of intimately knowing the truth, being the truth in relationship with God and others, and living the truth before the world around us, starting in our own families. This is God's plan to know, to be, and to live his truth and naturally impart that living and transformational truth to others.[3]

You are living out your life in a time when the thought of absolute truth is being mocked. In fact, truth has become relative based on who the person is and the surrounding circumstances. As a result,

---

[3] Josh and Sean McDowell, The Unshakable Truth: How You Can Experience the Twelve Essentials of a Relevant Faith, (Eugene: Harvest House Publishers, 2010) 41.

huge moral and ethical decisions are made based upon what one *feels* he should do. That has disaster written all over it!

All of God's Word is available to you—not just the first five books of the Bible. God's Word is truth; and as such, it is our final source for faith and practice. Do you want to honor Jesus in the way you treat your wife, in the way you parent your children, in the way you live with integrity both at work and at home, and in the way you fulfill God's purpose for your life? You must think and act biblically. Richard Mayhue commented:

> Who could imagine that the three-pound human brain—comprising one hundred billion neurons and that handles ten thousand thoughts daily, regulates over 103,000 heartbeats every twenty-four hours, coordinates over 23,000 breaths a day, and controls over six hundred muscles—would also play such a central role in determining the nature and value of our lives? Yet this is exactly what Scripture teaches in Romans 8:5: "For those who live according to the flesh set their minds on the things of the flesh, but those who live according to the Spirit set their minds on the things of the Spirit."[4]

Is your mind centered on the Word of God? Do you allow God's truth to regulate what you think, how you feel, and what you do? Do not ignore what God has to say. Dedicate yourself to the systematic study of the Bible, and commit yourself to live in obedience to the truth of the Lord. The impact this will have on your life is off the charts, and it is highly practical.

For instance, the next time you are out of town on business and the loneliness of the hotel is suffocating, what you do with the remote control can make you or break you. Mindlessly flipping through the channels might seem harmless, but Satan has a way of taking an image and arresting your attention. Like David, you can fall for the lie that no one will ever know what you do, or you can turn your attention to God's truth. Focus on Jesus' words in the Sermon on the Mount: "You have heard that it was said, Do not commit adultery. But I tell you, everyone

---

[4] John MacArthur with The Master's College Faculty, Think Biblically: Recovering A Christian Worldview, (Wheaton: Crossway Books, 2003) 38.

who looks at a woman to lust for her has already committed adultery with her in his heart" (Matthew 5:27–28).

Pornography is a relationship killer. Take immediate action by turning off the TV, opening the Bible and reading it, and living out the truth. Other suggestions would be to listen to podcast sermons, praise music, or read that Gospel-centered book you have been meaning to read. Precaution is a great strategy. Why not pack an eight-by-ten picture of your wife and children and set it on top of the TV when you check in to your room. Now *that* is motivation to live in purity!

Lunch with a female coworker may seem to be innocent. What can be wrong with talking about business? Over time, your friendship with this lady grows, and you think about her more and more. You can feel yourself going down a road that God has explicitly marked "no entrance." How will you respond? Will you allow your feelings to dictate your actions, or will you focus on the Word and allow its principles to determine what you do? Whatever you do, stay out of tempting situations!

You have at your disposal all the eternal truth that David had at his disposal but, unlike him, you can draw wisdom and direction from the rest of the Old Testament and all of the New Testament. Think on Jesus' words to the Pharisees—"'Haven't you read,' He replied, 'that He who created them in the beginning made them male and female,' and He also said: 'For this reason a man will leave his father and mother and be joined to his wife, and the two will become one flesh? So they are no longer two, but one flesh. Therefore, what God has joined together, man must not separate'" (Matthew 19:4–6). This absolute truth, properly applied, can literally pull you back from the brink of disaster.

A word of warning might be appropriate here. Never allow yourself to develop a close friendship with a member of the opposite sex! Focus on your relationship with your Lord, with your wife, and with solid Christian men with whom you can develop a healthy accountability. Learning to think and act biblically is vital for every man who loves his Lord and his family.

TRANSFORMATION

Some coaching principles apply to other areas of life also. One such principle that has enormous implications for men is this one—*you play like you practice.* If you ever played on an athletic team, I would imagine that you heard that line numerous times. During the week of practice leading up to the game, you went over the game plan time and time again. Your coach wanted you to react properly in every given game situation. He wanted you to be a winner!

You need to know that this same principle—*you play like you practice*— is highly relevant as you shift from your role as an athlete to your role as the leader of your family. God the Father wants you to be a winner. There are some things you need to know about your Lord.

Some Facts You Need to Know

First, God flat out loves you! Get this. Nothing you ever do or fail to do will cause Him to love you less or to love you more. He loves you perfectly and permanently. Here's how Paul put it in his letter to the Romans: "For I am persuaded that not even death or life, angels or rulers, things present or things to come, hostile powers, height or depth, or any other created thing will have the power to separate us from the love of God that is in Christ Jesus our Lord!" (Romans 8:38–39). Right now, your mind may be swirling with this question: can we really know for sure that God loves us? Again, listen to Paul's words: "But God proves His own love for us in that while we were still sinners, Christ died for us!" (Romans 5:8). This might be an appropriate time to ask you a significant question.

Have you come to the point in your life where you really want to change from the inside out? God proved His love for you by sending His Son, Jesus Christ, to die for *all* your sins on the cross. The Savior paid your penalty with His own blood. God forgives sin on the basis of what His perfect Son did, and not on the basis of what you do. The story does not end with the sacrificial death of Jesus.

God raised Jesus from the dead. He is a living Savior and Lord who has the power to change lives even today. Your response to this splendid good news is crucial. Are you willing to turn from your sin (repent) and place your faith in Jesus as your personal Lord and Savior? Jesus' promise to every person who follows through is breathtaking: "I assure you: Anyone who believes has eternal life" (John 6:47).

Many of you have been followers of Christ for some time. First, you need to know that God will never stop loving you even if you have a moral train wreck like King David. However, He loves you too much to leave you like you are. He will discipline you when you step outside of His eternal purpose for your life. The reason is simple. He wants you to be like Jesus and to experience the abundant life that He has promised to those who believe in Him.

Second, God will forgive you. Not one of us is perfect. Either you will sin by doing something God has clearly forbidden, or you will sin by failing to do something that God has clearly indicated He wants you to do. Obviously, a true believer does not lose his relationship with the Lord, but fellowship with Him is hampered. What you do next is important.

Forgiveness is much more than just saying you are sorry. The Bible reveals two keys to biblical forgiveness: "The one who conceals his sins will not prosper, but whoever confesses and renounces them will find mercy" (Proverbs 28:13). You must *confess* your sin to God. That is exactly what David did when he failed so miserably (Read Psalms 32 and Psalms 51). Wait now; there is something else that God requires. You must *renounce* your sin. This is a synonym for repentance. As Jack Taylor so aptly put it in a sermon, a sinning believer must *admit it* and *quit it.* Follow the teaching of this verse and the Lord will pour out His compassion and mercy on your life. Once again, you can enjoy fellowship with the Lord Jesus. Conquering sin may not always be immediate and this straight forward, but there is hope with a repentant heart.

Third, God will restore you. Do not think for a minute that your heavenly Father will keep you in His doghouse for the rest of your life. The good news of the Gospel is simply this: your life can still make an eternal difference. Never allow yourself to lose hope for the future.

Yes, David had to bear the consequences of his sin. His heart must have broken every time he saw the impact his sin made in the lives of those he loved and those he led. God forgave him, restored him to the kingship of Israel, and used him in a remarkable way. How amazing is that!

God still has a clear purpose for your life. He wants to transform you into the image of His Son so that you will bring honor and glory to Him. Although you would probably like to speed up this process, God's Word indicates that the Holy Spirit will be working in and through your life until you step into eternity. Love Jesus with all your heart and serve Him faithfully so that your life can make an eternal difference.

Some Actions You Need to Take

First, devote yourself to abiding in Jesus. He said, "I am the vine; you are the branches. The one who remains in Me and I in him produces much fruit, because you can do nothing without Me" (John 15:5). You, as a believer, are to *remain* in Jesus (other translations use the word *abide*). How do you do that? Carve out time in your day when you commit yourself to the consistent practice of reading the Bible and praying. When you read the Bible, the Lord speaks to you. When you pray, you speak to the Lord. That healthy dialogue results in both spiritual growth and spiritual fruitfulness. Without a doubt, this spiritual discipline is one of the most important steps you can take as you seek to live within the glory of God's eternal purpose for your life.

Second, be filled with the Holy Spirit. Do not be frightened by this reference to the Spirit of God. Did you know that every born-again believer has received the Holy Spirit who now indwells his life? On top of that, each believer is commanded to be filled with the Spirit. Paul wrote, "And don't get drunk with wine, which leads to reckless actions, but be filled by the Spirit:" (Ephesians 5:18). Simply put, the filling of the Holy Spirit answers the question, who is in charge? Your life will be vastly improved when you surrender control of your life to the Spirit of God and allow Him to live His life through you.

Jesus never intended for any of His disciples to live the Christian life by charting their own course or by exerting their own strength. Living to please Jesus requires that we die to ourselves and live in total dependence on the Holy Spirit's guidance and supernatural power. Paul's words offer great clarity on this subject: "Finally, be strengthened by the Lord and by His vast strength" (Ephesians 6:10). Are you not thrilled that supernatural power is available to you every single moment of your life? You can meet every challenge that comes your way, and you can live in such a way that both the Father and the Son are honored.

Third, do not panic when you are tempted. By the way, you *will* be tempted. How you handle temptation is crucial. Paul, writing under the inspiration of the Holy Spirit, gave us a wonderful promise. He wrote, "No temptation has overtaken you except what is common to humanity. God is faithful, and He will not allow you to be tempted beyond what you are able, but with the temptation He will also provide a way of escape so that you are able to bear it" (1 Corinthians 10:13). Read that carefully. You must not cave in to temptation because you assume that no one else has ever faced the monster you are facing. Trust me; you are not the first man to face sexual temptation, an ethical temptation, or some other kind of temptation. God is faithful, and He sovereignly controls how the enemy can tempt you. Furthermore, He always provides a way of escape. What a mighty God we serve!

The next time you face temptation please keep this verse at your fingertips. You do not have to fall for the sin that Satan uses to entice you. Look for the door of escape your Lord will provide for you, and run with a sprinter's speed out of that door!

David's life offers hope for every man. Following Jesus does not mean that you have to be perfect. God can take any man who is serious about his spiritual life and use him in some amazing ways. Failure never has to be final. Paul's words provide a great closing challenge: "Therefore, my dear brothers, be steadfast, immovable, always excelling in the Lord's work, knowing that your labor in the Lord is not in vain" (1 Corinthians 15:58).

QUESTIONS FOR REFLECTION

Personal Reflection

1. Have you repented of your sin and placed your faith in Jesus Christ?

2. Do you have a passion to know Christ and to serve Him?

3. If you have failed, have you dealt with your sin in a biblical way? Explain your answer.

4. Are you abiding in Christ? If so, how? If not, why not?

Group Reflection

1. What have you learned about God's character and attributes in this chapter?

2. What biblical promises mean the most to you and why?

3. Will God give a man another chance to get it right if he blows it? What if he blows it repeatedly?

4. How hard is it to forgive yourself even after you know that God has forgiven you? How do you handle your feelings of guilt, shame, or defeat?

Dr. Chuck Herring has been senior pastor at Collierville First Baptist Church, in Collierville, Tennessee, since 2003. His ministerial background includes being pastor at New Hope Baptist Church in Folsom, Louisiana; pastor at Mullins Station Baptist Church in Memphis, Tennessee; and senior pastor at First Baptist Church in Richland, Mississippi. He earned his BS and EdM from Mississippi State University in Starkville, Mississippi, and his MDiv and DMin from New Orleans Baptist Theological Seminary in New Orleans, Louisiana. Originally from Saltillo, Mississippi, Chuck is married to Darlene, and their family includes daughter, Heather, and her husband, Vic; their son, Zac; and their grandchildren, Cade and Aynsley. God did not call him to preach until he was thirty years old. Chuck has coached football, taught in three different schools, and he still love athletics.

7

PURSUING GOD THROUGH CONFESSION AND RESTORATION

INTRODUCTION

Two events in the life of David provide examples of how to respond to sin in one's life by pursuing God through confession and restoration. The first event is probably the most well-known—his adultery with Bathsheba (2 Samuel 11). The second event involved his unauthorized census of the people (1 Chronicles 21).

David tried to hide the sins related to his adultery with Bathsheba for almost a year, but "God does not allow His children to sin successfully."[1] Hiding his sin was not the right response. David had to be prompted to deal with his sin, so God sent the prophet Nathan to confront him (2 Samuel 12). This confrontation prompted David to respond appropriately to his sin by pursuing a right relationship with God through confession and repentance. Out of that experience, he wrote Psalms 51 to express his heartfelt confession, genuine repentance, and deep desire for God's restoration. David wrote, "Purify me with hyssop, and I will be clean; wash me, and I will be whiter than snow. Let me hear joy and gladness; let the bones you have crushed rejoice. Turn you face away from my sins and blot out all my guilt. God, create a clean heart for me and renew a steadfast spirit within me. Do not banish me

---

[1] Warren W. Wiersbe, Be Worshipful (Psalms 1-89), (Colorado Springs: Victor, 2004) 187.

from Your presence or take Your Holy Spirit from me. Restore the joy of Your salvation to me, and give me a willing spirit" (Psalms 51:7–12).

When David ordered an unauthorized census of the people, God afflicted Israel. Once again, after a period of time, David recognized his sin and said to God, "I have sinned greatly because I have done this thing. Now, please take away Your servant's guilt, for I've been very foolish" (1 Chronicles 21:8). After disciplining both David and the people, God instructed David to build an altar and offer sacrifices on the very place that would one day become home to the temple. This place was none other than Moriah, the place where God had instructed Abraham to offer his son, Isaac, as a sacrifice and the place near where Jesus would one day be crucified.[2]

How should the one who desires to live as "a man after God's own heart" in this twenty-first-century world deal with sin in his life? How should he respond to sin in his life after he has ignored God's commands and purposes to chart his own course? Should he try to hide from God, make excuses for his sin, or even blame others for his sin (Genesis 3:8–13)? The answer is obviously, "No!" Like David, sin in one's life must be confronted with God's help. Like David, he must confess his sin without making excuses and demonstrate sincere repentance.

Only after he has confessed his sin, repented of his sin, and received God's forgiveness, can God begin His work of restoration in the man who desires to walk according to God's ways. Of course, there may be lingering consequences of sin to deal with on a regular basis. Yet, there is the promise that God can bring something good out of failure. There is the hope that God can take the man who is humbled by his sin and restore him to usefulness in His kingdom. The assignment may be different, but there is the opportunity to help others understand that forgiveness and restoration are possible.

TRIALS

Because of his unfaithful choices, David experienced trials both publicly and privately. For instance, David's servants observed his

---

[2] J. A. Thompson, 1 & 2 Chronicles: New American Commentary, Vol. 9, (Nashville: Broadman and Holman, 1994) 163.

suffering as he watched the child born out of his adultery with Bathsheba die (2 Samuel 12:14–18). When David ordered the unauthorized census of the people, the elders joined David in mourning as he watched the Lord send a plague on Israel, which resulted in the death of seventy thousand men (1 Chronicles 21:14). The private, inward trials that David experienced are also clearly expressed in Scripture. In these two life events, David experienced at least three inward trials that are worth noting.

David experienced the burden of his sin

After David committed the sin of adultery with Bathsheba, he experienced great internal anguish as he tried to hide his sin. "When I kept silent, my bones became brittle from my groaning all day long. For day and night Your hand was heavy on me; my strength was drained as in the summer's heat" (Psalms 32:3–4). This burden is also expressed in Psalms 51:3–4, "For I am conscious of my rebellion and my sin is always before me. Against You—You alone—I have sinned and done this evil in Your sight. So You are right when You pass sentence; You are blameless when You judge."

David was very much aware of his sin. It was "always there, a shameful waking nightmare."[3] He had a "living, never-at-rest, painful consciousness of it."[4] He came to understand that the unfaithful choices he made were indeed sin. While his sin dramatically affected others, he came to understand that his sin was first and foremost rebellion against God. Therefore, God was "right" and "blameless" to punish his sin. This burden of sin radically affected his fellowship with God.

David experienced the guilt of his sin

David's decision to number the people had far-reaching effects upon those around him. In 1 Chronicles 21:8, David said to God, "I have

---

[3] Michael Wilcock, The Message of Psalms: Psalms 1–72 (The Bible Speaks Today), (Downers Grove, IL: IVP, 2001) 186.

[4] Bruce K. Waltke and James M. Houston with Ericka Moore, The Psalms as Christian Worship: A Historical Commentary, (Grand Rapids: Eerdmans, 2010) 470.

sinned greatly because I have done this thing. Now, please take away Your servant's guilt, for I've been very foolish." While the exact nature of David's sin in this case is unclear, it may have had something to do with his motive for taking the unauthorized census.[5] Regardless of the nature of his sin, God considered his action "evil" (1 Chronicles 21:7). David experienced guilt as a result of his choice and acknowledged that it was "foolish."

David witnessed firsthand the effects of his sin on others as seventy thousand men died in the plague God sent on Israel. As God had an angel positioned between heaven and earth to destroy Jerusalem, David cried out to God, "Wasn't I the one who gave the order to count the people? I am the one who has sinned and acted very wickedly. But these sheep, what have they done? My Lord God, please let Your hand be against me and against my father's family, but don't let the plague be against Your people" (1 Chronicles 21:17). David experienced the guilt associated with the effects his sin had on those around him.

David experienced fear because of his sin

In Psalms 51:11 David wrote, "Do not banish me from Your presence or take Your Holy Spirit from me." 1 Samuel 16:13 says that when Samuel anointed David as king, "the Spirit of the LORD took control of David from that day forward." The very next verse says, "Now the Spirit of the LORD had left Saul" (1 Samuel 16:14). It is highly possible that David feared the same thing would happen to him because he had willfully disobeyed God and sinned.[6]

Most commentators agree that David did not fear the loss of his salvation and relationship with God, but instead feared losing God's power in his life. He knew he could not live a holy life without God. David needed the presence of God's Spirit every moment of every day if he ever hoped to overcome future temptations to sin and continue to be "a man after God's own heart."[7]

---

[5] Andrew E. Hill, 1 & 2 Chronicles: NIV Application Commentary, (Grand Rapids: Zondervan, 2003) 294.

[6] Wilcock, 187.

[7] James Montgomery Boice, Psalms: An Expositional Commentary, Vol. 2 (42–106), (Grand Rapids: Baker, 1996) 433.

Application for Life

For the man committed to walk in the ways of God, there will be times when he falls short of God's standards and sins in some way. When this happens, the best plan is to quickly confess the sin, repent of it, receive God's forgiveness, and move forward. There may be some lingering consequences from the sin, but God can make him stronger and wiser in the process.

However, this response is not always the response when a man sins. Often he will try to hide the sin or think that it is no big deal. Hiding his sin and not dealing with it swiftly creates a secret burden that he must carry daily. It produces an inner turmoil, drains him of his energy, and is always in the back of his mind.

Along with this heavy burden, the man of God who does not confront his sin will also experience waves of guilt and the fear that his "secret sin" will affect those around him. While he may try to convince himself that his sin only affected him, sin almost always affects others in some way. There is the very real possibility that his sin will affect his relationship with his spouse, his children, and others close to him. If his sin is of a more serious nature, when it becomes public, it will also affect his ability to lead within his community, workplace, and church. Most of all, his unwillingness to deal with his sin will affect his relationship with God.

The good news is there is hope. David experienced the burden, guilt, and fear associated with his sin. However, he also began to pursue God's help and seek His restoration. The one who desires to be "a man after God's own heart" would do well to follow his example.

TRUTH

These two life events provided numerous opportunities for David to demonstrate his obedience and faithfulness to God. However, they also became opportunities for David to ignore God's leading in his life. The account of David's unauthorized census in 1 Chronicles 21 is particularly instructive.

David's Disobedience (1 Chronicles 21:1–7)

First Chronicles 21:1 begins with the declaration that Satan "incited David to count the people of Israel." The parallel account in 2 Samuel 24:1 says, "The Lord's anger burned against Israel again, and He stirred up David against them to say: 'Go, count the people of Israel and Judah.'" While at first glance these verses seem to contradict one another, they are both true. God allowed Satan to tempt David in the matter of the unauthorized census.[8] Yet, the fact that David was tempted by Satan to conduct the census does not absolve him from guilt in the matter.[9] Verses 1–7 indicate at least two mistakes David made in this matter.

He did not inquire of the Lord (vv. 1–2). There is no indication anywhere in this passage that David took the time to inquire of the Lord whether he should take a census. While the purpose of this census is not given, there were two basic reasons to conduct a census in his day: to levy taxes or to register adult men for military service (Hill 293).[10] Therefore, a census itself is not necessarily evil, but in this case, many commentators believe the problem was the motive behind the census—pride.

He did not listen to the counsel of others the Lord placed in his life (vv. 3–7). Joab questioned David's order and his motive in verse 3, "Why does my lord want to do this? Why should he bring guilt on Israel?" David ignored the counsel of those closest to him. Verse 6 indicates that Joab even adjusted David's order because of his belief that the unauthorized census was not a good decision and was "detestable to him." Verse 7 clearly states, "This command was also evil in God's sight, so He afflicted Israel." Warren Wiersbe points out, "Whatever the cause, the Lord was displeased (1 Chronicles 21:7), but He permitted Joab and his captains to spend the next nine months and twenty days counting the Israelites twenty years old and upward who were fit for military service. Sometimes God's greatest judgment is simply to let us have our own way."[11]

---

[8] Warren W. Wiersbe, Be Restored (2 Samuel & 1 Chronicles), (Colorado Springs: Victor, 2002) 156.

[9] Hill, 293.

[10] Joyce G. Baldwin, 1 & 2 Samuel: An Introduction and Commentary, Tyndale Old Testament Commentary, (Downers Grove, IL: IVP, 1988) 295.

[11] Wiersbe, 157–158.

David's Obedience (1 Chronicles 21:8–17)

When God afflicted Israel, David must have immediately recognized the affliction as a response from God to his unauthorized census. Once he recognized his action was wrong, once he was confronted with his sin, David responded accordingly.

He confessed his sin (v. 8). David said to God in verse 8, "I have sinned greatly because I have done this thing. Now take away Your servant's guilt, for I've been very foolish." Once again, Wiersbe's comments are helpful: "When he confessed his sins of adultery and murder, David said, 'I have sinned'; but when he confessed his sin of numbering the people, he said, 'I have sinned greatly.' Most of us would consider his sins relating to Bathsheba far worse than the sin of numbering the people, and far more foolish, but David saw the enormity of what he had done. David's sins with Bathsheba took the lives of four of David's sons (the baby, Amnon, Absalom, and Adonijah) plus the life of Uriah; but after the census, God sent a plague that took the lives of seventy thousand people. The Lord must have agreed with David that he had indeed sinned greatly."[12]

He trusted in God's mercy (vv. 9–13). After David's confession, God sent the prophet Gad to him to offer him three choices of discipline: "three years of famine, or three months of devastation by your foes with the sword of your enemy overtaking you, or three days of the sword of the Lord—a plague on the land, the angel of the Lord bringing destruction to the whole territory of Israel." David's response in verse 13 is a response of trust in God's mercy: "I'm in anguish. Please let me fall into the Lord's hands because His mercies are very great, but don't let me fall into human hands." J. A. Thompson notes, "David did not choose but cast himself on the mercy of God. This is a sign of true repentance—he left all in God's hands and did not seek to determine the way that might have seemed easiest for him."[13]

He repented of his sin (vv. 14–17). Even though David had confessed his sin and thrown himself upon the mercy of God, God still allowed David to see and experience the consequences of his sin as seventy thousand Israelite men died. As a sign of his genuine repentance,

---

[12] Wiersbe, 158.
[13] Thompson, 162.

verse 16 records that "David and the elders, clothed in sackcloth, fell down with their faces to the ground." For a second time, David cried out in confession accepting full responsibility for his sin in verse 17: "Wasn't I the one who gave the order to count the people? I am the one who has sinned and acted very wickedly. But these sheep, what have they done? My Lord God, please let Your hand be against me and against my father's family, but don't let the plague be against Your people."

David's Renewed Surrender and Restored Favor (1 Chronicles 21: 18–30)

David continued to demonstrate renewed obedience to God beyond his confession, trust, and repentance.

He obeyed God's direction (vv. 18–19). Gad once again appeared to David with a command to "set up an altar to the Lord on the threshing floor of Ornan the Jebusite" (v. 18). David obeyed the Lord's direction promptly.

He offered God his all (vv. 20–24). When Ornan offered to give David the threshing floor for nothing, David refused and said, "No, I insist on paying the full price, for I will not take for the Lord what belongs to you or offer burnt offerings that cost me nothing" (v. 24). After his repentance, David fully surrendered himself to the Lord and was willing to sacrifice in order to please Him. He would not offer the Lord less than his best regardless of what it cost him.

He enjoyed God's favor once again (vv. 25–30). Verse 26 describes what happened after David secured the place for the altar: "He built an altar to the Lord there and offered burnt offerings and fellowship offerings. He called on the Lord, and He answered him with fire from heaven on the altar of burnt offering." The fire sent from heaven, which consumed David's offering, demonstrated the fact that God had accepted his repentance and his sacrifice.[14] David now, once again, enjoyed the favor of God.

It is interesting to note what 2 Chronicles 3:1 says about the place on which this altar was built: "Then Solomon began to build the Lord's

---

[14] J. Barton Payne, edited by Frank E. Gaebelein, 301–562, 1 & 2 Chronicles. In Vol. 4 of The Expositor's Bible Commentary, (Grand Rapids: Zondervan, 1988) 409.

temple in Jerusalem on Mount Moriah where the Lord had appeared to his father David, at the site David had prepared on the threshing floor of Ornan the Jebusite." The place where the Lord had instructed David to build this altar, after his sin of conducting the unauthorized census, was the very place the Lord instructed Solomon to build the temple. It was Mount Moriah, the place the Lord had instructed Abraham to offer his son Isaac as a sacrifice and the place near where Jesus would one day die on Calvary.[15] Wilcock makes this observation: "This is not of course an excuse, still less a justification, for sinning. To say that we may 'do evil that good may come,' and 'continue in sin that grace may abound,' is no part of a biblical faith. But when we do sin, God can take that sin and its evil effects and transmute them into something which will contribute to his glory."[16]

Application for Life

Bryan Chapell wrote about an event that happened during the Great Awakening. Jonathan Edwards was presiding over a prayer meeting of eight hundred men. A woman sent a message asking the men to pray for her husband. The note described a man who had become unloving, prideful, and difficult. Edwards read the message in private and then, thinking that perhaps the man described was present, made a bold request. Edwards read the note to the eight hundred men. Then he asked if the man who had been described would raise his hand, so that the whole assembly could pray for him. Three hundred men raised their hands.[17]

The man of God must be willing to seek the Lord about everyday decisions of life. He must be willing to listen to the wise counsel of the godly men in his life. He must be willing to listen as the truth of God's Word and the Holy Spirit convicts him of sin. When he does identify sin in his life, he must be willing to deal with it, and not hide it. He must be willing, like the men of Edward's day, to confess his sin, trust God's

---

[15] Thompson, 163.
[16] Wilcock, 91.
[17] Bryan Chapell, "Holiness by Grace." Preaching Today, 2001, http://www.preachingtoday.com/illustrations/2001/october/13342.html, accessed 1 October 2013.

mercy, repent of the sin, and not return to it. He must be willing to completely surrender to the Lordship of Christ in his life if he hopes to experience the restoration God offers. One thing is certain: there can be no restoration until there is first confession.

TRANSFORMATION

For the "man after God's own heart" who desires to experience the transforming power of God in his life and is ready to face the sin in his life, Psalms 51 provides a clear path for restoration and healing. In this psalm, David pours out his heart to God. He is real. He is honest. He holds nothing back. The "man after God's own heart" would do well to follow in his steps.

Seek God's Forgiveness (Psalms 51:1–2)

David began his journey toward restoration and healing by seeking God's forgiveness. He asked God to "be gracious" to him by appealing to His "faithful love" and "abundant compassion." David recognized his utter dependence upon the grace, love, and mercy of God, and on the basis of these unchanging attributes of God, he sought forgiveness for his sin. As David pursued God, he acknowledged that his actions were sin and as such, he desperately needed God's forgiveness. He did not simply pray, "God forgive me." He was very specific in his request for forgiveness.

First, he needed God to "blot out" his "rebellion." When David described his sin as "rebellion," he admitted that he had willfully chosen to cross a forbidden boundary set by God.[18] He needed God to "blot out" his sin and "wipe it away" like one would erase writing from a book.[19] Second, he needed God to "wash away" his "guilt." Guilt has already been mentioned as one of the things David experienced because

---

[18] James Montgomery Boice, Psalms: An Expositional Commentary, Vol. 2 (42–106), (Grand Rapids: Baker, 1996) 426.

[19] Derek Kidner, Psalms 1–72: Tyndale Old Testament Commentary, (London: IVP, 1973) 207.

of his sin. His request for God to wash away his guilt literally meant to "launder," and brings to mind the required process in that day of "treading, kneading, or beating to make the garment clean with lye and soap." David needed God to do the difficult work of washing away his guilt as if it were a spot on a soiled garment.[20]

Third, he needed God to "cleanse" him from his "sin." When David used the word *sin*, he was admitting that he had "fallen short" and "missed the mark" of God's high standard in the same way that an arrow might fall short of its target.[21] David needed God to cleanse him so that he would be clean once again. David sought God's forgiveness by asking Him to remove his sin completely, to remove the stain of sin in his life, and grant him the opportunity for a fresh, clean start.

Confess Known Sin (Psalms 51:3-6)

David did more than just acknowledge his actions needed God's forgiveness. He confessed his awareness that his actions were indeed sin. In fact, he was constantly "conscious" of his sin because it was "always before" him. David took ownership of his sin when he described it as "my rebellion" and "my sin." He did not try to hide it anymore, and he did not try to blame others for it. He simply confessed it and agreed with God about it. This open admission of sin and accepting of responsibility are sure signs of true repentance.

While David's sin certainly affected others, his sin was most directly against God and therefore God was justified in disciplining him for his sin. The more David pondered his sin, the closer he came to fully understanding his guilt. He was a sinner because of the choices he had made, but he was also a sinner by nature. He was in no way trying to absolve himself of any guilt by pointing to his sin nature. He was simply stating the truth behind his actions. He was taking full responsibility. He knew his character was flawed. What he needed was for God to work in him in such a way as to bring about the integrity in his inner person that God desired.

---

[20] Waltke and Houston, 469.
[21] Boice, 426.

Receive God's Cleansing (Psalms 51:7–9)

David desired to receive God's cleansing in three ways. First, he wanted God to purify him with hyssop so that he would be clean. The word *purify* translated can mean, "to cleanse" or literally "de-sin." In other words, David wanted "to have his sin completely purged away."[22] The use of "hyssop" referred to either the practice of cleansing of a leper by sprinkling with the sacrificial blood seven times, or the ritual cleansing of those who had come into contact with a dead body. In both cases, after the cleansing, the person was declared clean.[23] The phrase "wash me, and I will be whiter than snow" is simply another way to speak of the cleansing David desired.

Second, David wanted to experience "joy and gladness" once again. The effects of David's sin had taken its toll on him, and these emotions were hard to come by. Instead, he was experiencing the effects of his sin, which was more like the pain associated with crushed or broken bones. As Gerald Wilson points out, "Crushed bones may 'rejoice,' but they may never be whole again. The effects of sinful choices and evil living may never fully depart from us, any more than the effects of long-term alcoholism or drug addiction or AIDS contracted from an uncontrolled life of sexual addiction. Our rejoicing may have to be expressed alongside the lasting consequences of our sin."[24]

Third, because David realized his sin had affected his relationship with God, he asked God to "turn Your face away from my sins." He, once again, asked God to "blot out" his sin and remove it from His memory. This hope caused David to write in Psalms 103:12, "As far as the east is from the west, so far has He removed our transgressions from us."

---

[22] Boice, 428.

[23] Kidner, 209–210.

[24] Gerald H. Wilson, Psalms Volume 1: NIV Application Commentary, (Grand Rapids: Zondervan, 2002) 782.

Experience God's Renewal (Psalms 51:10–12)

After seeking God's forgiveness, confessing his sin, and receiving God's cleansing, David wanted to experience God's renewal in his life. He desired to experience renewal in several ways.

First, David had experienced the terrible effects of sin in his life, and he did not want to fall into sin again. He also knew his heart was the source of his trouble, but he was unable to change his own heart.[25] He needed God to "create a clean heart" in him. The Hebrew word for "create" in this verse is same word used in Genesis 1 when God created the heavens and the earth. It is a word used to describe only what God can do. Only He can create something out of nothing.[26] By using the word "create," David asked God to do in him only what God Himself could do. In essence, David was asking God for a miracle.[27]

Second, David wanted God to "renew a steadfast spirit within" him. David was a "man after God's own heart," one completely surrendered to God's will. However, in his sin with Bathsheba, his spirit of complete surrender to God's purpose wavered. So David petitioned God to "renew" his former resoluteness of purpose.[28]

Third, he did not want God to "banish him" from His presence or "take" His Holy Spirit from him. As mentioned earlier, David experienced fear because of his sin. He had seen the effects of God removing His spirit from Saul, and he feared God might do the same to him. He did not want God to remove His hand of favor from him. He wanted to continue to experience God's very real presence with him at all times.

Fourth, he wanted God to "restore the joy of Your salvation." The fact that David asked for so many things in this psalm is an indication that he had become acutely aware of how much he had lost when he gave into sin.[29] David had not lost his salvation, but he had lost the "joy" of his salvation and lost his close fellowship with God. John Phillips believes "much of the depression in the lives of Christians today is caused by sin. It may be flagrant sin, hidden away somewhere in the

---

[25] Warren W. Wiersbe, Be Worshipful (Psalms 1–89), (Colorado Springs: Victor, 2004) 188.
[26] Boice, 432.
[27] Kidner, 209–210.
[28] Waltke and Houston, 476.
[29] H. C. Leupold, Exposition of Psalms, (Grand Rapids: Baker, 1977) 405–406.

past, gnawing away at the conscience. It may be something spitefully said, some fit of temper indulged, or some lie told. Sin causes depression."[30]

Fifth, he wanted God to give him a "willing spirit." David wanted God to conform his will to His will. David wanted God to work in his life in such a way that he would want the same things that God wanted. David was surrendering himself, again, to work in cooperation with God's purpose and plan for his life.

Teach God's Ways (Psalms 51:13)

After seeking God's forgiveness, confessing his sin, asking for God's cleansing, and desiring to experience God's renewal, David expressed his desire to teach other rebellious sinners like himself the way to restored fellowship with God. He could teach them about the temptations and dangers of sin. He could teach them about the burden, guilt, and fear sin brings into a person's life. He could also teach them about the need for forgiveness, confession, cleansing, and renewal. He could teach them about God's power to bring about restoration in the life of "a man after God's own heart."

Application for Life

Max Lucado wrote, "Confession does for the soul what preparing the land does for the field. Before the farmer sows the seed, he works the acreage, removing the rocks and pulling the stumps. He knows that seed grows better if the land is prepared. Confession is the act of inviting God to walk the acreage of our hearts. 'There is a rock of greed over here, Father; I can't budge it. And that tree of guilt near the fence? Its roots are long and deep. And may I show you some dry soil, too crusty for seed?' God's seed grows better if the soil of the heart is cleared.[31]

---

[30] John Phillips, Exploring the Psalms, Vol. 1 Psalms 1–88, (Neptune, NJ: Loizeaux Brothers, 1988) 409.

[31] Max Lucado, In the Grip of Grace: You Can't Fall Beyond His Love, (Dallas: Word, 1996) 122.

These two events in the life of David demonstrate that restoration after sin and failure is possible. When David sinned, he did the hard work of clearing his heart of debris. He responded by pursuing God through confession and repentance. When God saw that David's confession was sincere and his repentance was genuine, He then granted forgiveness and began the process of restoration.

The modern man after God's own heart, who desires to be used of God, must live a life of integrity. He must guard against temptation and sin in his life. He must flea when temptation presents itself. He must not allow sin to take up root in his life. When he is overcome by sin, then he must do the hard work of preparing his heart for God's use again.

Today's man of God must be willing to deal with secrets sins like lust and pornography. He must be willing to ask other men to hold him accountable in order to protect against unhealthy attractions and potential affairs. He must remove those obstacles that stand in his way of being the honorable husband, faithful father, and loving leader his family needs. He must establish priorities that allow him to lead his family to worship weekly and serve sacrificially through the local church.

First John 1:9 promises, "If we confess our sins, He is faithful and righteous to forgive us our sins and to cleanse us from all unrighteousness." The man after God's own heart must be open and honest about his confession of sin. He must determine to repent and make a clean break with sin. He must humbly come before the Lord asking for forgiveness, cleansing, renewal, and restoration to be useful in God's kingdom. If he is willing to be transparent with God, then God can continue transforming him into a man after His own heart.

QUESTIONS FOR REFLECTION

Personal Reflection

1. Are you experiencing the burden, guilt, and fear of a hidden sin?

2. What is hindering you from confessing your sin?

3. Are you willing to do the hard work of repentance?

4. Do you desire to experience God's forgiveness and restoration?

Group Reflection

1. What are some of the greatest fears related to hidden sin in the life of a leader?

2. Why is it so difficult for leaders to confess their sin publicly?

3. What are some of the signs of genuine repentance?

4. Do you know of someone who has experienced restoration after a very public sin? If so, how were they able to receive God's forgiveness and move forward?

Trent Bullock has been the senior pastor of First Baptist Church in Paris, Tennessee, since February 2009. He is a graduate of Union University (BA) in Jackson, Tennessee; New Orleans Baptist Theological Seminary (MDiv) in New Orleans, Louisiana; and The Southern Baptist Theological Seminary (DMin) in Louisville, Kentucky. Trent Bullock has been married to his wife, Lori, since April 24, 1993, and they have two daughters, Meredith and Megan. He enjoys spending time with his family, watching sports (especially University of Kentucky basketball), and reading.

8
THE NEED FOR SPIRITUAL ACCOUNTABILITY

INTRODUCTION

Reading of David's affair with Bathsheba and the subsequent choices he made is akin to watching a train wreck happen. Throughout the narrative, it appears that the train is going to wreck. When the train does in fact wreck, the damage is worse than anticipated. The unfortunate story of David and Bathsheba and the tragic actions that follow demonstrate the collateral damages of sin and the consequences. Even more unfortunate, the entire affair could have been prevented.

David's decision to stay home led him to see beautiful Bathsheba bathing on her rooftop across the way one afternoon. Seeing her led him to inquire about her. His inquiry about her eventually led him to call to her and then sleep with her. In an effort to cover up the matter, David compounded things by having Bathsheba's husband, Uriah, murdered. This sordid tale of spiraling sin—lust, adultery, deception, murder—is told in 2 Samuel 11. After Uriah's death, Bathsheba grieved over her dead husband and was brought to David's house where she married him and eventually bore him the son who was conceived in sin. Yes, David had made all the wrong choices, and a concluding period is put on the end of the chapter as it ends: "But the thing that David had done displeased the LORD" (2 Samuel 11:27).

After all that David did, at the end of 2 Samuel 11, the reader must wonder, "Is David going to get away with murder, in addition to all his other sinful choices? While chapter 11 concludes with the Lord's thoughts about the situation, chapter 12 begins with God's action. The Lord steps in by sending the prophet Nathan to David. Through the relationship of these two men and through the accountability that Nathan provides for David in the aftermath of this fiasco, God opens David's eyes to his sin, convicts him of his sin, and forgives him. Here, God's working in David's life is exemplified through David's relationship with Nathan.

God often uses earthly relationships as an avenue through which He moves. At the beginning, God said, "It is not good that man should be alone" (Genesis 2:18). Not only did God provide Adam and Eve for one another in creation, He provides believers today with friends and mentors as He does a work of sanctification in their lives. "His divine power has granted to us all things that pertain to life and godliness . . ." (2 Peter 1:3); and God has given Christians the precious gift of accountability for the purpose of life and godliness.

God often brings people together to help one another in challenging times—challenging times that are often results of poor personal choices, as was the case with David. God also puts believers in the paths of other believers so that difficult experiences might be avoided and so that God will indeed be honored through righteous living.

In the Christian community, and especially within the context of Christian accountability, train wrecks do not have to happen. They are often avoidable. Through God's gift of accountability, believers are able to walk together, share life together, resist temptation together, and pursue the things of God together. Why go it alone? May David and Nathan's relationship from yesterday provide helpful instruction for today.

TRIALS

Believers find joy in the midst of, or after overcoming, temptation because they know that the testing of faith produces steadfastness, and steadfastness results in maturity (James 1:2–3). Whether trials are brought on by our own poor choices or consequences of others' sin, they can, in fact, result in spiritual maturity and deeper joy. David's trials were direct consequences of his own decision making. Like Eve looking at the forbidden fruit, David saw that Bathsheba was a delight to the eyes. He desired her, and he sent for her so that he might have her. When he initially saw her on the roof that afternoon, David probably never would have imagined things leading to adultery and deception. Murder was probably the furthest thing from his mind. As

Walter Scott penned in his 1808 poem "Marmion," "Oh what a tangled web we weave, when first we practice to deceive!"[1]

Laying out the three-step process of sin in a person's life, James says, "each person is tempted when he is drawn away and enticed by his own evil desires. Then after desire has conceived, it gives birth to sin; and when sin is fully grown, it gives birth to death" (James 1:14–15). This sad process plays itself out in David's life as he makes one bad choice after another.

A reason is not given for David's decision to stay at home during that season when kings go out to battle, but in the end, he probably wished he had made the decision to battle. Instead, he lay around the house, and at one point, his eyes wandered to a nearby rooftop where a woman named Bathsheba was bathing. Rather than immediately looking away, he allowed his eyes to linger lustfully on her beautiful body. The look evolved into a desire for Bathsheba, and brazenly, David gave instructions for someone to go get her so that his sexual desires might be fulfilled. Thinking that his encounter might have only been a momentary rendezvous, David then heard the three words that no adulterer wants to hear: "I am pregnant." Talk about an unwanted pregnancy!

In an effort to cover up adultery with Bathsheba, David arranged for Uriah to come home from war and spend the night with Bathsheba in hopes that Uriah might think that the child growing in Bathsheba's womb belonged to him. Uriah's integrity during wartime caused him to abstain from sexual relations with his wife that night. Even after David got Uriah drunk, Uriah still did not sleep with Bathsheba. David's deceptive ploy had been averted again.

In a seeming act of desperation, David wrote Joab the next morning with instructions that Uriah be placed at the front of the fiercest fighting so that he might be killed. Sadly, David's plan succeeded. Upon hearing of Uriah's death, Bathsheba was deeply grieved. David must have found himself relieved—at least for a little while.

---

[1] Sir Walter Scott, Scottish author and novelist (1771–1832), Marmion, Canto vi. Stanza 17.

Living in a Sex-Saturated Society

A man pursuing God in today's society may not experience trials like those brought on by adultery and murder, but they do experience some of the same challenges faced by David.

For David, Bathsheba was on the roof. For men today, sexual temptation is everywhere. Images of scantily clad women and other sexually suggestive sights are all around. In days gone by, Ricky and Lucy Ricardo were fully clothed and slept in separate beds. Today, a sensitive parent must continuously monitor the television to ensure that children in the house do not see the sexual images that frequently appear on television and computer screens. While a follower of Christ may say with the psalmist, "I will not set anything worthless before my eyes. I hate the practice of transgression; it will not cling to me" (Psalms 101:2–4), living with such integrity is more challenging than ever in today's society.

Today, it would be rare to see a woman bathing on a roof. Instead, sexual temptations come to men in other ways—through television, movies, the Internet, and more. The world of the early twenty-first century is indeed a sex-saturated and sex-crazed world. According to FamilySafeMedia.com, men ages thirty-five to forty-nine are the largest consumers of Internet pornography. In fact, 42.7 percent of all Internet users view pornography sites. There are 4.2 million pornographic websites on the World Wide Web, and every second, $3,075.64 is spent on pornography.

Covering Sin

David's trials only increased as he sought to cover his wrongdoing. Without God's prophet by his side, David continuously made wrong decisions. As David sought to cover the sin with Bathsheba, and as he lived without the benefit of men of integrity in his life, David's situation went from bad to worse.

Generally speaking, men often live with a desire to project a certain image, and sometimes this desire means trying to hide whatever perceived warts may exist. Men sometimes want others to think that all is well. There are no needs, and there are no deficiencies. Men before David, and many who have come after him, have sometimes desired to project an image of faultlessness and self-sufficiency. Men are often hesitant to admit weaknesses—much less failures. Since the days of Adam and Eve, men have pursued isolation rather than community. They have run from others rather than to those God has placed around them. Men often shut down to themselves rather than open up to others.

Like David, men often compound personal difficulties by refusing to own up to mistakes. There is often a resistance to being transparent about trials and challenges. Men characteristically retreat into the inner world of private thoughts and are hesitant to share with others. Often, men see church as merely a service to be attended rather than a community to be joined.

The pressure a man feels from others can, oftentimes, make him want to appear strong, confident, extraordinary, and together, which can lead a man to pursue isolation from those who are nearest. When a man refuses to maintain transparent relationships with others, there is a greater tendency to slide slowly into sin. When a man does not take advantage of a surrounding Christian community, poor choices that lead to ongoing trials can multiply.

TRUTH

Truth is on the line these days. While many Christians believe in objective and absolute truth, others find themselves cynical and skeptical about any kind of truth claim. Moreover, many downright deny the existence of objective truth. It is often common to hear people talking about what they "feel" rather than what they "believe." An outcry was heard worldwide as Americans denounced the attacks of September 11, 2001, as "atrocious," "horrific," and "evil." America heard no one question the absolute nature of the truth that it is undeniably wrong for people to use passenger planes to crash into buildings and kill innocent people. In the aftermath of the September 11 terrorist attacks, no one appeared on television upholding the feelings and preferences of the terrorists. Sadly though, Americans often see truth as merely a matter of preference that is loosely tethered to their own particular feelings on a given day.

At all times, but particularly in the midst of trials, it is essential for believers to look at life in a proper perspective. The follower of Christ looks upon the challenging experiences of life in light of the unchanging truth, which is revealed in Scripture. Believers do not see truth through the lens of experiences. Instead, believers look at experiences through the lens of truth. Right is right—regardless of what one might experience. Wrong is wrong—regardless of how one might feel. Truth is not based on how we feel.

God is the Source of all truth. In fact, apart from God, one cannot know truth as it is meant to be known. Proverbs 9:10 says, "The fear of the LORD is the beginning of wisdom, and the knowledge of the Holy One is insight." One grows in truth through a proper acknowledgment of God. Jesus told followers, "If you abide in my word, you are truly my disciples, and you will know the truth, and the truth will set you free" (John 7:31–32). Jesus boldly declared to Thomas, "I am the way, and the truth, and the life" (John 14:6). God has given the truth to us so that we might know him and so that we might live accordingly.

Sowing and Reaping

The ebb and flow of personal choices and resulting consequences is an ongoing reality of life. Paul calls this cyclical pattern sowing and reaping. He says, "Do not be deceived; God is not mocked, for whatever one sows, that will he also reap. For the one who sows to his own flesh will from the flesh reap corruption, but the one who sows to the Spirit will from the Spirit reap eternal life" (Galatians 6:7–8).

Just as a farmer prepares the ground and plants seeds, which produce a crop, so also a person's choices are individual plantings that eventually rise up and bear fruit for all to see. Sow tomato seed, and tomato plants eventually rise out of the ground. Plant cottonseed, and cotton soon will be seen budding from the growing plants that emerge from the ground. The presence of a field with rows and rows of soybeans is sure evidence of sowing—and not just any sowing, but a sowing of soybeans.

The biblical principle of sowing and reaping is universal. Whether acknowledged or not, reaping will always follow sowing. In a certain moment, a particular act may not seem to have consequences, but be very sure—there is a consequence for every action. Where sowing has occurred, reaping will take place. The reaping may not occur immediately. Consequences may not follow right away, but one may be guaranteed of a future reaping. First Samuel 11 recounts David's encounter with Nathan, but prior to and following this significant chapter, the reader realizes that David's initial choices of what to sow reaped a harvest that he never would have imagined.

Ralph Waldo Emerson once said in the *Selected Writings of Ralph Waldo Emerson*, "Sow a thought and you reap an action; sow an act and you reap a habit; sow a habit and you reap a character; sow a character and you reap a destiny."[2] With the sordid trail of lust, adultery, deception, and murder in David's recent past, David might have grieved over Absalom's death with a regretful remembrance of that quick, desirous look at Bathsheba one afternoon. David's choices, which plunged him deeper into sin, began with one little look. What a life-changing destiny reaped from a simple thought.

Some imagine that the principle of sowing and reaping does not apply to the use of today's Facebook and Twitter. Words are often sown (typed and tweeted) to the world without consideration of what those words might consequentially reap for the author. Last year, Olympians in Britain learned the hard way that the principle of sowing and reaping applies to even the words they shared in the Twitter sphere. One United States athlete was reprimanded by her coach when she used social media to publicly question the knowledge of a soccer analyst. Police arrested a teenager for "malicious communication" tweeted about Britain's synchronized diver, Tom Daley. The Swiss Olympic team expelled an athlete who tweeted racist and threatening comments about an opposing team after losing a soccer match. Imagine how many years the athlete worked, trained, practiced, hoped, and anticipated playing before the world at the 2012 Olympics—only to see it all vanish with the hasty movements of a few quick thumb strokes!

Actions have consequences. Although it seemed harmless when David's eyes wandered from his roof to the roof where Bathsheba bathed, he made the conscientious choice to watch her rather than look away. David's desire for the woman resulted in an inquiry. Upon finding out that the bathing woman was Bathsheba, the wife of Uriah the Hittite, David boldly, "sent messengers and took her, and she came to him, and he lay with her" (2 Samuel 11:4). One verse later, we read that Bathsheba sent word to David that a baby had been conceived (2 Samuel 11:5).

---

[2] Ralph Waldo Emerson, Selected Writings of Ralph Waldo Emerson, (New York: Penguin Group, 1965).

David's situation goes from bad to worse. Joab is called by David for the purpose of requesting Uriah, Bathsheba's wife. David tries to deceive Uriah by allowing him to take a break from fighting so that Uriah might go home and sleep with Bathsheba—and thereby believe that the child growing in Bathsheba's belly belonged to Uriah. David's deceptive ploy to lead Uriah to sleep with Bathsheba failed a second time—even when David led Uriah to become drunk.

Now David was desperate. To cover his lust, adultery, and deception, David turned to murder. Indeed, David believed that desperate times called for desperate measures. So, he instructed Joab to place Uriah on the front lines of the fiercest fighting and for Joab to draw away from Uriah so that Uriah might be killed. This time, David's plan worked. And while David must have experienced temporary relief by removing Uriah from the scene, David now had blood on his hands.

His desperate attempt at manipulation, to cover his lust, adultery, and deception, eventually leads to murder. Many of life's trials simply happen—as a result of no one's doing. Sometimes, people face trials that have been brought on because of what others may have done. Like David, there are times in life when trials faced are direct results of personal choices made. David chose to lust, and David's choice to lust resulted in the consequence of desire. David chose to act on his desire to have Bathsheba, and David's choice to lay with Bathsheba resulted in pregnancy. David chose to act on his desire to deceive Bathsheba's husband, and David's choice to deceive Uriah led to Uriah's unwillingness to lay with Bathsheba. David made a decision to kill Uriah, and David's decision to get rid of Uriah led him to cold-blooded murder. The tragic murder of an innocent man started with a seemingly harmless look at a naked woman. On the roof that afternoon, David probably never would have imagined murdering another person. Some often use the phrase, "If looks could kill." In the case of David and Bathsheba, David's look did kill. As the consequences of David's choices piled up in his life, the initial look proved to be merely a first step toward David's murder of Uriah.

If believers lived with a greater awareness of the principle of sowing and reaping, perhaps fewer trials might occur. It is challenging to think about sowing and reaping in the midst of temptation. When consequences are unimaginable and distant, it often seems that one's sowing will never reap fruit. The downward descent of David's choices from a lustful look to blatant murder is a vivid example that "whatever a man sows he will also reap" (Galatians 6:6).

TRANSFORMATION

Sharpening One Another

Romans 12:2 says, "Do not be conformed to this age, but be transformed by the renewing of your mind, so that you may discern what is the good, pleasing, and perfect will of God." God brings about transformation through the mind when the principles of God's Word are lined up with the practices of daily living. Understanding the principle of sowing and reaping means that one must think carefully about any action, realizing that for every action, there is a corresponding result. In addition to the principle of sowing and reaping, God has also provided believers with the principle of sharpening. "Iron sharpens iron, and one man sharpens another" (Proverbs 27:17). Here, the writer of Proverbs compares men to iron and equates the sharpening of one another to the sharpening that takes place when iron rubs against iron.

Reading about Nathan's encounter with David might cause one to bristle at such direct and in-your-face dialogue. Sure, Nathan told a story about a rich man, a poor man, and a little ewe lamb, but Nathan audaciously confronted David with those four harsh words, "You are the man!" There is even an exclamation point at the end of the sentence, and a superscription at the top of 2 Samuel 12 reads, "Nathan Rebukes David." Although David committed heinous acts in the previous chapter, the scene between Nathan and David is almost too raw to behold.

Nathan comes across as brazen and bold. One might imagine Nathan with a Type A personality and a get-things-done-no-matter-what attitude. God sent Nathan to speak prophetically, in a less-than-compassionate way about David's sin. Moving further into the chapter, one realizes that David does in fact listen to Nathan and responds by saying, "I have sinned against the LORD" (2 Samuel 12:13). With a blend of grace and conviction, Nathan responds, "The LORD also has put away your sin; you shall not die. Nevertheless, because by this deed you have utterly scorned the LORD, the child who is born to you shall die" (2 Samuel 12:13–14).

Those who avoid confrontation may not enjoy the story of David and Nathan. Though confrontation is often avoided, God has placed believers in community with one another so that they may have accountability as well as fellowship. There is no such thing as a Lone Ranger Christian. Personal solitude is indeed a spiritual discipline, but no one rides alone in the Christian faith. Christians pursue community with one another and realize that confrontation is sometimes necessary for the sake of personal holiness.

Throughout Scripture, believers are called to live in community and are reminded of the importance of personal relationships through the many "one another" passages. ". . . be at peace with one another" (Mark 9:50); ". . . wash one another's feet" (John 13:14); "Love one another" (John 15:17); "Show family affection to one another with brotherly love" (Romans 12:10); ". . . be in agreement with one another" (Romans 12:16); ". . . pursue what promotes peace and what builds up one another" (Romans 14:9); "live in harmony with one another" (Romans 15:5); ". . . serve one another through love" (Galatians 5:13); "Carry one another's burdens" (Galatians 6:2); "Be kind and compassionate to one another, forgiving one another" (Ephesians 4:32); ". . . encourage one another" (1 Thessalonians 4:18); "confess your sins to one another and pray for one another" (James 5:16); ". . . be hospitable to one another" (1 Peter 4:9); and "clothes yourselves with humility toward one another" (1 Peter 5:5).

One of God's greatest gifts is the gift of community—the gift of one another. For a piece of iron to sharpen another piece of iron, those two pieces must touch. They must contact one another. In the same way, a Christian man is sharpened by his contact with another Christian man. Personal relationship within the Christian community is the design of God.

Believers are often tempted to avoid others in the church or in a Christian community. A fear of what others might think often causes one to recoil and resist getting close to others—much less making contact with others. A child who has done wrong often hides from his parents before the parent even knows of the child's behavior. Adam and Eve's wrong choices led them to flee from God's presence. While David might have dreaded seeing Nathan coming his way, Nathan's coming to David was a gift of grace. David may have thought that he had much to hide—lying, cheating, murdering—but through his encounter with Nathan, David experienced transforming restoration. David experienced personal repentance as well as God's forgiveness and fellowship.

Those who walk into a believer's life—much like Nathan did—are gifts from God. Second Samuel 12 clearly states that the Lord sent Nathan to David. Nathan may have wrestled over and prayed about going to David, but Scripture states that God is the One who sent Nathan to David.

Nearly 7 billion people swarm the planet, and God knows each one. His knowledge of all things does not prevent Him from knowing the smallest detail of our lives. God was intimately aware of everything David was experiencing. God knew of David's need to repent, and He was eager to forgive. For this reason, God sent Nathan into David's life at the appropriate time to confront him concerning his sin. Indeed, it is the kindness of God that leads people to repentance (Romans 2:4). With a simple story of a rich man who unjustly took a poor man's only lamb, the Lord used Nathan to bring David to a place of repentance concerning his sin. Nathan spoke into David's life and David listened. David received Nathan as a gift from God who would help him think about his actions from God's perspective.

Listening to Others and Seeing Life Through the Lens of God's Word

David listened to Nathan with an understanding that life's experiences are to be interpreted through the lens of God's Word. Modern society tends to prioritize personal feelings and experiences over universal principles and truth. Subjective feelings often trump objective realities. Truth and error as well as good and evil are often cast aside in light of how a person may feel at a particular time. What is considered true for one person may be considered false by another. The believer is one who does not look at the truth of God's Word in light of experiences; rather, all of life's experiences are evaluated in light of the truth of God's Word. Through Nathan, David saw experiences in light of the truth that Nathan spoke.

Believers today have a wonderful resource in one another. Christian friends are often sent from God to step into the lives of others and provide godly perspective, encouragement, and hope. David acknowledged his sin because of Nathan's direct words. With starkness, David admitted, "I have sinned against the LORD" (2 Samuel 12:13). While consequences surely followed because of David's choices and while David would eventually experience the death of his own son, David began a return to spiritual health as Nathan spoke godly words of restoration, encouragement, and hope. "The LORD has put away your sin; you shall not die" (2 Samuel 12:13–14).

Hebrews 10:24–25 says, "And let us be concerned about one another in order to promote love and good works, not staying away from our worship meetings, as some habitually do, but encouraging each other, and all the more as you see the day drawing near." Oh, the power of those words—"not staying away." Men are often tempted to stay away: to stay away from the worship gathering, to stay away from other men, to stay away from family. The flesh of a man often craves isolation, but the Spirit leads believers into community and accountability with one another. Like David and Nathan, followers of God need one another. And because of God's good gift of community, followers of God have one another. Perhaps this is the reason the writer of Hebrews said, "But encourage each other daily, while it is still called today, so that none of you is hardened by sin's deception" (Hebrews 3:13).

Christians realize that righteousness flourishes in community. God's people have consistently gathered together throughout the years. Sometimes those gatherings have taken place in large arenas. For years, Christians have huddled together in small groups in church classrooms. Christians who face persecution have often found themselves secretly meeting together in basements in the dark of night. Often two or three Christians gather over breakfast to share their struggles and hopes together, to pray together, and to encourage one another in their pursuit of the Christian life.

One who resists Christian accountability and community does so at great risk. While a believer never plans to fall into sin, it is important to realize that every person is "prone to wander" and "leave the God I love."[3] For this reason, believers must pursue accountability with brothers and sisters who commit to share the Christian walk, and who ask those tough questions that aid in the fight against ungodliness, and which spur one another on to love and good deeds.

With the prayer that unbelievers may come to salvation in Christ, Christians are eager to share the Gospel with those who do not know God.

---

[3] Taken from the hymn, "Come Thou Fount of Every Blessing," written by Robert Robinson. Public domain.

In addition to an articulation of the Gospel, Christians are also committed to a demonstration of the Gospel. One of the greatest demonstrations of the Gospel is the Christian's personal accountability relationship.

In addition to sitting under the regular teaching of the Word of God, an accountability relationship with another believer is key for health and success in faithful living. Too often, men are self-deceived, thinking that mere attendance at church is sufficient for walking with God. It is quite possible to attend church regularly and resist God-ordained community by remaining in personal isolation. Personal relationships and spiritual accountability often serve as the lifeblood through which the grace of God flows. David realized this through the encounter with Nathan. Nathan was willing to go to David. David was willing to receive Nathan. When believers help one another apply the truths of God's Word to the everyday choices of life, there is growth and godliness.

The 1980s witnessed a boom in the church growth movement in America. Hordes flocked to mall-like buildings and gathered in large numbers to sit under the preaching of God's Word and to participate in a myriad of Christian activities. Christians can be thankful for this special time in American history when scores of people came to Christ and grew in relationship with God. As American evangelicalism is currently experiencing many new church starts, it is important to realize that health and vitality are often found not in the size of corporate Christian gatherings, but the nature of personal Christian relationships. Regardless of the size of the crowd, the follower of Christ must intentionally pursue and maintain relationships with Christian brothers and sisters who cultivate the application of Christian truth with the context of personal relationships of spiritual accountability.

A Christian friend who is willing to walk beside another person and speak godly words of honesty and hope is one of God's greatest gifts. Proverbs 11:14 says, "Without guidance, people fall, but with many counselors there is deliverance." No one is immune from falling. Regardless of how long one may have been a Christian, no one has the ability to see perfectly. A person who understands the inability to live well and pursue God in isolation seeks out community and works to incorporate accountability into daily living. The follower of Christ understands that accountability afforded by guidance from faithful believers is not simply a good thing. For Christian living, accountability is an essential thing.

QUESTIONS FOR REFLECTION

Personal Reflection

1. What kind of Christian community do I have?

2. How would an accountability friend assist me in my walk with God?

3. How can I assist someone else?

4. In terms of community and accountability, how might I best pursue God's design?

Group Reflection

1. Why are men often resistant to personal relationships of spiritual accountability?

2. How does a relationship of spiritual accountability practically work in today's society?

3. How can the church encourage relationships of spiritual accountability?

Todd Brady serves as vice president for University Ministries at Union University. A graduate of Union University, Southwestern Baptist Theological Seminary, and Southern Baptist Theological Seminary, Todd has served as a student minister, college minister, and local church pastor. Todd and his wife, Amy's, greatest earthly joy is being parents to their five sons. They are members of First Baptist Church in Jackson, Tennessee. He is a popular speaker, teacher, and writer.

9

CONSIDERING THE EFFECTS OF IMMORALITY ON THE FAMILY

INTRODUCTION

The next few pages serve to examine the impact of immoral behavior upon the family. In the life of David, Israel's finest king, a story of soap-opera proportions points to the principle effects of sexual immorality upon the entire family. In the book of James, we read, "You ask and don't receive because you ask wrongly, so that you may spend it on your desires for pleasure" (James 4:3). We do not know what David's requests to God were just before this dark time in his life, but seeing the commands he gave his subjects, we can imagine his prayer life was nonoperative, or at least defective. Why else would the man who had everything commit adultery and conspire to have his mistress' husband killed?

These embarrassing events begin with a seemingly bored David acting in total selfishness. In today's vernacular, someone could ask, "David, what were you thinking?" He certainly was not thinking of his family, and his choice for instant gratification led him to other ghastly choices he made against his God, his subjects, his family, and even warriors willing to die for him. He was trying to conceal his first wicked choice.

You Are an Adult Now!

Whether a rural church, small-town church, storefront church, suburban church plant in the Midwest, or an urban church, some things never change. God and His glorious Gospel never change, and people are generally the same everywhere. Opposite of virtuous consistencies, however, are some bitter redundancies that can have a devastating effect. For example, picture an individual desperately trying to cope with the bitter harvest of his sexual sin. Whatever sexual allurement they could not live without now poisons, with nocuous consequences, some of God's greatest gifts in his life and those of his family members.

Some would say they have been weak, while others would say they have been wicked. They have been both of these, but they have also been selfish. Like a toddler who wants a toy or a teenager who wants his own life, grown people for whom Jesus died sometimes want what they want; they just do not like what they get—consequences. I want to say to them, "You are an adult; act like one!" One thing I cannot say is, "God will always remove the earthly consequences of sin."

Gospel Hope

Despite seemingly unbearable consequences, God never abandoned David. The very fact that David responded to God's prophet: "I have sinned against the LORD" and Nathan responded, "The LORD has taken away your sin . . ." (1 Samuel 12:13), demonstrates the existence of an authentic relationship between David and the Lord. In approaching how sexual immorality affects the family, it is important to know that restoration is possible. After having repented, David pleaded, "Restore the joy of Your salvation to me . . ." (Psalms 51:12a). There was hope even for David, yet his life demonstrates that earthly consequences that follow moments of sinful pleasure often remain and are horrific to bear. Correspondingly, there is hope today for those caught in this ancient trap. God forgave David of adultery and murder, among other things. Is God a pushover? No. David was forgiven and restored because of another King who would come. This King would not have a seventy-five-pound gold crown as did David; He would have a crown of thorns!

TRIALS

David's Family Fallout

We can only imagine how we would react in David's situation. Reminiscent of a trashy, daytime talk show, David's family is plagued with the saga of more sexual immorality, not to mention murder, rebellion, and even treason against the king. Second Samuel chapters 11–18 is a depressing depiction of a family gone wild. In fact, through Nathan the prophet, God indicated what some of the consequences of David's sin would be:

> I am going to bring disaster on you from your own family: I will take your wives and give them to another before your very eyes, and he will sleep with them publicly. You acted in secret, but I will do this before all Israel and in broad daylight . . . David responded to Nathan, "I have sinned against the LORD." Then Nathan replied to David, "The LORD has taken away your sin; you will not die. However, because you treated the LORD with such contempt in this matter, the son born to you will die." Then Nathan went home. The LORD struck the baby that Uriah's wife had borne to David, and he became ill (2 Samuel 12:11–15).

It is evident that David realized none of his sin was invisible to God. The painful reality for David was that he was also learning that God is never unconcerned with sin.

The Lord Struck the Child

Nathan prophesies that several tragedies will occur in David's life, but that God will forgive David and spare his life. The first prophecy to come true is the last one recorded in Nathan's dialogue with David, which is the death of David's illicitly conceived son.

In modern evangelical circles, God has learned to "behave better" than striking innocent children with illness. At least an outsider to biblical interpretation might have this perception when overhearing a postmodern explanation of current calamity. How should twenty-first-century believers respond to these instant dismissals of modern-day tragedies having come from the hand of God?

First, know that God does not change. Malachi 3:6 records God declaring, "For I am the LORD, I do not change; therefore you are not consumed, O sons of Jacob."

Second, our faith today is based on revelation that was progressive in nature but is now complete in the Bible. It stands not on the evolution of religion but on God's inerrant Word. In other words, the prophet Nathan did not misunderstand and the prophet Samuel misreport ". . . the LORD struck the child that Uriah's wife bore to David, and it became ill." There are those who follow what is called "The History of Religions" approach, which originated from Germany in the late nineteenth century and remains popular today. In short, they would say that the Old Testament is not true history or revelation from God. It is, instead, legend mixed with some facts that have nothing to do with what actually happened or who God actually is. These facts, in their view, simply demonstrate an evolution of how the author and people of the day perceived God and the events of their lives.

Ultimately, one has to decide at this point if the Bible, and specifically the Old Testament, is authoritative and accurate. Though disbelieving the Scripture was not the source of David's downfall, doubting God's Word often is one of the pitfalls of many who find themselves in sexual immorality today. They think the Bible is passé or that God is a passive pushover.

A person struggling with sexual temptation and sin desperately needs to believe God's Word and take it seriously. Jesus told the two discouraged disciples on the road to Emmaus, "How unwise and slow you are to believe in your hearts all that the prophets have spoken!" (Luke 24:25). Jesus, while specifically making application of the messianic content of the Old Testament, more than inferred that the Old Testament is true revelation from God. The purpose in discussing the nature of Scripture at this point is to state emphatically that God did strike David's son with a fatal illness, and a person's sin today could elicit a like response from God! David fasted, prayed, and stayed awake for seven days trying to change God's mind. God was silent and the child died. We cannot begin to speculate on God's reasoning for allowing this child to die. One can only imagine the stigma this child would have faced in Israel. As king of Israel, David's life was an example to the nations, which set the course for God's people.

This episode in David's life gives us reason to pause and contemplate the character of God. David's life clearly carried the weight of messianic promise and enjoyed the security of God's covenant relationship. While it is difficult to understand why this child's life was lost, we cannot allow it to distort a biblical understanding of the character of God. While it is hard to grasp, God sometimes allows the innocent to lose their lives. Is that not the case of Jesus, His own Son? God the Father required the life of His innocent Son for the benefit of others. So, while the purpose behind this child's death is not entirely clear, we must choose to trust the sovereign and loving hand of God who was clearly at work. Glimpses of God's goodness are evident in David's declaration in 2 Samuel 12: 23b, "I'll go to him, but he will never return to me," which is implies that he would see his son in paradise one day.

Incest, Rape, and Murder

After his son dies and he comforts his wife, life moves on for David. Bathsheba gives birth to the heir to his throne, Solomon; there are great military victories; and David gets some new bling, not to mention a new prison labor force (see 2 Samuel 12:24–31). Then the unthinkable happens. David's firstborn, Amnon, began to lust after his half sister, Tamar. (Maacha was the mother of Tamar and Absalom, while Ahinoam was Amnon's mother.) Remember, David has not only taken many wives, which surely complicated his life, but he has also killed to get Bathsheba. The apostle Paul said, "Don't be deceived: God is not mocked. For whatever a man sows he will also reap" (Galatians 6:7). This law of the harvest, as it is called by many today, was to David what gravity is to a man without a parachute. David saw a beautiful, naked woman and had to have her for himself. Now Amnon sees not another man's wife but his half sister and begins to lust after her. Through a wicked cousin of Amnon's, Tamar is put in a position where Amnon can easily take advantage of her. He rapes her. What a bitter harvest of sin!

Wait; there is more. Tamar is thrown out like a piece of trash by Amnon after he steals her virginity and dignity. Two years later, Tamar's brother Absalom gets Amnon drunk on wine and then orders his assistants to kill him. This long-since fermented revenge brings the harvest of murder to David's family. David now has bloodshed between his own sons. Unfortunately, David's life illustrates perfectly James' statements concerning the origin of human conflict. James asked and answered, "What is the source of the wars and the fights among you? Don't they come from the cravings that are at war within you? You desire and do not have. *You murder and covet and cannot obtain.* You fight and war. You do not have because you do not ask. You ask and don't receive because *you ask wrongly, so that you may spend it on your desires for pleasure*" (James 4:1–3, emphasis added).

David is seeing his own selfish sins find expression in his family. The pattern is now moving generationally.

David Loses a Third Son

While Absalom may have rationalized his sin of killing Amnon, he certainly had no justification for attempting to steal his father's kingdom. Nathan's prophecy and the law of the harvest come to fruition in every way. Absalom momentarily steals away the kingdom. Not only does he exile his father, he sets up a tent on the roof of the palace where he allows the public to observe him spending the night with each of his father's ten concubines whom David had left behind (see 2 Samuel 16:21–22). While David is marching around with his loyalists preparing to face Absalom, Shimei, one of King Saul's relatives, assails David with curses and stones. One of David's men says, "Why should this dead dog curse my lord the king? Let me go over and cut his head off!" (2 Samuel 16:9b). With profundity, David affirms that the man is within God's will to curse him! The Bible leaves us this and other hints, which imply that David understood why these things were happening to him and to his family.

Remember, Nathan had proclaimed that David's sexual sin was in private but that he would be mocked publicly (2 Samuel 12:11). Though David was able to take his kingdom back from his rebellious and treasonous son, it would be at the cost of Absalom's life. Although some might be inclined to see this as a happy ending, David certainly did not. In fact, his advisors prompt him to reciprocate the loyalty of his people lest they not stand with him on future occasions of battle. The Bible says,

> But the King hid his face and cried out at the top of his voice, "My son Absalom! Absalom, my son, my son!" Then Joab went into the house to the king and said, "Today you have shamed all your soldiers—those who rescued your life and the lives of your

> sons and daughters, your wives and your concubines. You love your enemies and hate those who love you! Today you have made it clear that the commanders and soldiers mean nothing to you. In fact, today I know that if Absalom were alive and all of us were dead, it would be fine with you! Now get up! Go out and encourage your soldiers, for I swear by the LORD that if you don't go out, not a man will remain with you tonight. This will be worse for you than all the trouble that has come to you from your youth until now!" (2 Samuel 19:4–7).

What a powerful prophetic truth that is experienced so profoundly in David's life. The Word of God, as proclaimed through Nathan, was as true in times of judgment as in times of blessing.

TRUTH

Taking to Heart What Comes After

Author Randy Alcorn tells of meeting a man who had previously been a Christian leader but had lost his ministry and witness due to sexual sin. Alcorn remembers: "He paused only for a moment, then said with haunting pain and precision, 'If only I had really known, really thought through and weighed what it would cost me and my family and my Lord, I honestly believe I would never have done it.'" Following this encounter, Alcorn and a friend of his independently compiled lists of what it would cost them to fall. They then combined their lists, which are as follows:

- Grieving my Lord; displeasing the One whose opinion most matters
- Dragging into the mud Christ's sacred reputation
- Loss of reward and commendation from God
- Having to one day look Jesus in the face at the judgment seat and give an account of why I did it
- Forcing God to discipline me in various ways

- Following in the footsteps of men I know of whose immorality forfeited their ministry and caused me to shudder (List of these names)
- Suffering of innocent people around me who would get hit by my shrapnel (a la Achan)
- Untold hurt to Nanci, my best friend and loyal wife
- Loss of Nanci's respect and trust
- Hurt to and loss of credibility with my beloved daughters, Karina and Angela ("Why listen to a man who betrayed Mom and us?")
- If my blindness should continue or my family be unable to forgive, I could lose my wife and my children forever
- Shame to my family ("Why isn't Daddy a pastor anymore?"; the cruel comments of others who would invariably find out.)
- Shame to my church family
- Shame and hurt to my fellow pastors and elders (List of names)
- Shame and hurt to my friends, and especially those I've led to Christ and discipled (List of names)
- Guilt awfully hard to shake—even though God would forgive me, would I forgive myself
- Plaguing memories and flashbacks that could taint future intimacy with my wife
- Disqualifying myself after having preached to others
- Surrender of the things I am called to and love to do—teach and preach and write and minister to others. Forfeiting forever certain opportunities to serve God. Years of training and experience in ministry wasted for a long period of time, maybe permanently
- Being haunted by my sin as I look in the eyes of others, and having it all dredged up again wherever I go and whatever I do
- Undermining the hard work and prayers of others by saying to our community "this is a hypocrite—who can take seriously anything he and his church have said and done?"
- Laughter, rejoicing, and blasphemous smugness by those who disrespect God and the church (2 Samuel 12:14)
- Bringing great pleasure to Satan, the enemy of God
- Heaping judgment and endless problems on the person I would have committed adultery with
- Possible diseases: gonorrhea, syphilis, chlamydia, herpes, and AIDS (pain, constant reminder to me and my wife, possible

infection of Nanci, or in the case of AIDS, even causing her death, as well as mine)

- Possible pregnancy, with its personal and financial implications, including a lifelong reminder of sin to me and my family
- Loss of self-respect, discrediting my own name, and invoking shame and lifelong embarrassment upon myself

"These are only some of the consequences. If only we would rehearse in advance the ugly and overwhelming consequences of immorality, we would be far more prone to avoid it. May we live each day in the love and fear of God" (emphasis original).[1]

Through this sobering exercise, Alcorn has reminded his readers, "So, whoever thinks he stands must be careful not to fall" (1 Corinthians 10:12). Some may be reading and thinking that the egregious act of sexual sin is beneath them. Watch out! Bob Reccord stated in his book *Beneath the Surface*, "a national ministry leader outside the United States recently told me he estimates that at least 50 percent of the pastors in his country have toyed with Internet pornography and a confidential survey was conducted among 350 men from a dozen evangelical denominations, which found 64 percent struggle with sexual addiction . . ."[2] At this point, a barrage of current statistics could be given. What is the point? Sex, illicit sex, is everywhere. David was tempted as are all. Adrian Rogers said, "The sin of immorality is not one we are instructed to fight. It is one we have been told to flee. Run from that compromising situation. *Saturate that place with your absence.*"[3] David and untold millions have not fled. They have had a bitter harvest because they hung around and thought they could handle it.

---

[1] Randy Alcorn, "Deterring Immorality by Counting Its Cost." Eternal Perspective Ministries, 12/31/2009, accessed September 30, 2013, http://www.epm.org/resources/2009/Dec/31/deterring-immorality-counting-its-cost.

[2] Robert Reccord, Beneath the Surface, (Nashville, TN: B&H Publishing, 2002) 11.

[3] Adrian Rogers, Adrianisms, (Memphis, TN: Love Worth Finding, 2006) 114.

Twin Inescapable Truths and Triple the Understanding

If there are two things clear in these passages of Scripture, they are that David neither escaped the earthly consequences and earthly judgment of his sin, nor did he forfeit the love and presence of the Lord. As families deal with the aftermath of sexual immorality, they must understand three facets of recovery and restoration: First, the aftermath may linger for years; David's did. Second, as was with David, God's presence and love remain, and He longs to restore His fallen children. They must return to what brought them into God's family in the first place—grace through the Gospel of Jesus. Third, anything less than absolute brokenness and repentance will bring false hope and false recovery. In fact, disingenuous apologies may demonstrate that one claiming to follow Christ is in fact unregenerate (not truly saved).

In light of these three facets, the Word of God provides a path to restoration. Here are steps, as evidenced in David's journey, that offer hope: Realize, Repent, Restore worship, and Remain humble.

Realize

In Psalms 51, we have David's very own, divinely inspired, prayer of realization, repentance, restorative worship, and humble pleas for the future. First, in verses 1–4, David, by implication and explicit appeal, demonstrates his realization that he had ultimately sinned against God and that God must act within his heart. David clearly realized his sin and God's remedy. Look at the first four verses: "Be gracious to me, God, according to Your faithful love; according to Your abundant compassion, *blot out my rebellion.* Wash away my guilt, and cleanse me from my sin. For I am *conscious of my rebellion* and my sin is always before me. *Against You—You alone—I have sinned and done this evil in Your sight.* So you are right when you pass sentence; You are blameless when you judge" (Psalms 51:1–4, emphasis mine).

Notice the word *conscious* in verse 3. Translated *know* in the New American Standard Bible and in the English Standard Version, and translated *acknowledge* in the New King James Version, Strong's designates it can even mean, "to comprehend."[4] David understood what he had done. The problem with many who want counseling for sexual sin, however, is that they merely want to cope with the consequences. In fact, recent trends see the Gospel disappearing from many churches and counseling sessions in favor of a seemingly more practical self-help message. D. A. Carson warns,

> Weigh how many presentations of the gospel have been "eased" by portraying Jesus as the One who fixes marriages, ensures the American dream, cancels loneliness, gives us power, and generally makes us happy. He is portrayed that way primarily because in our efforts to make Jesus appear relevant we have cast the human dilemma in merely contemporary categories, taking our cues from the perceived needs of the day. But if we follow Scripture, and understand that the fundamental needs of the race are irrefragably tied to the Fall, we will follow the Bible as it sets out God's gracious solution to that fundamental need; and then the gospel we preach will be less skewed by the contemporary agenda . . . If you begin with the Bible's definition of our need, relating perceived needs to that central grim reality, you are more likely to retain intact the gospel of God.[5]

Even in evangelical Bible-based churches, the Gospel is sometimes central only for knowing one's eternal destiny. Beyond this, Scripture is one unabridged testimony to humanity's need for Jesus the Messiah.

Not only does the absence of the Gospel dishonor Christ, it can damn the hearers. Just as people cannot be converted, or saved, if they do not realize their condition and God's grace, Christians who have sinned are not ready for restoration until they truly see their sin as needing God's remedy of grace.

David truly realized he had wronged God, but he began his prayer asking for mercy. It may sound trite or cliché, but the only hope for restoration for those caught in the trap of sexual immorality is to first be *truly* sorry, understanding that there are no more negotiations with God. He

---

[4] James Strong, A Concise Dictionary of the Words in The Hebrew Bible, (New York: Abingdon Press, 1890) 47.
[5] D. A. Carson, The Gagging of God, (Grand Rapids, MI: Zondervan, 1996) 221.

alone can heal based on His loving kindness (abundant compassion, HCSB), which is an Old Testament phrase equated with the New Testament idea of grace. One of the greatest proclaimers of God's Gospel, Charles Haddon Spurgeon of nineteenth-century Britain, said of Psalms 51:1:

> Pardon of sin must ever be an act of pure mercy, and therefore to that attribute the awakened sinner flies . . . What a choice word is that of our English version, a rare compound of precious things: love and kindness sweetly blended in one—"Lovingkindness." *According unto the multitude of thy tender mercies.* Let Thy most loving compassions come to me, and make Thou Thy pardons such as these would suggest. Reveal all thy gentlest attributes in my case, not only in their essence but in their abundance. . . . Obliterate the record, though now it seems engraven in the rock forever; many strokes of thy mercy may be needed, to cut out the deep inscription, but then Thou has a multitude of mercies, and therefore, I beseech Thee, erase my sins.[6]

David realized his need for forgiveness and restoration. His plea for God's graciousness harmonizes precisely with Paul's teaching in Ephesians 2, which affirms the hopeless, sinful, and dead state of people before God's grace in salvation. In fact, in Psalms 51:5–7, David confesses the origin of his costly mistakes—his origin as one born in sin. He then acknowledges that God wants inward transformation that only God can accomplish. "Indeed, I was guilty when I was born; I was sinful when my mother conceived me. Surely You desire integrity in the inner self, and You teach me wisdom deep within. Purify me with hyssop, and I will be clean, wash me, and I will be whiter than snow."

Even as David acknowledged his sin and neediness, he recognized God's ability and willingness to forgive. What a gracious picture of one who has dealt with such difficult circumstances resulting from his own sin.

---

[6] Charles H. Spurgeon, "The Treasury of David" The Spurgeon Archive, v. 2, accessed October 1, 2013, http://www.spurgeon.org/treasury/ps051.htm.

TRANSFORMATION

Repent

David's continued prayer for forgiveness leads to the next characteristic of restoration—repentance. While the word *repent* is not used in Psalms 51, the concept bleeds throughout the psalm. Repent is not an often-used word today. The principle of repentance indicates a turning away or change in direction. Jesus identified a lack of repentance among the religious leaders of the day when he exclaimed, "No I tell you; but unless you repent, you will all perish as well!" (Luke 13:3). So many today would love to save face during the aftermath of sexual immorality, but they do not want to repent. They may turn away from the act, but biblical repentance is more than that. So after realizing and owning the reality of sin, a biblical response would be godly sorrow for the sin that results in repentance.

Restore Worship

Notice David never even mentioned sexual immorality in Psalms 51, though he mentioned bloodshed. This is not to say he had not mentioned it to God (see 2 Samuel 12:13). The Bible is clear that we should specifically confess our sins even to our brothers and sisters in Christ (see James 5:16). The problem is that people not only endure the earthly consequences for their sexual immorality, they endure the cause of their sexual immorality. Read closely how David prays in Psalms 51:8–12:

> Let me hear joy and gladness; let the bones You have crushed rejoice. Turn Your face away from my sins and blot out all my guilt. God, create a clean heart for me and renew a steadfast spirit within me. Do not banish me from Your presence or take Your Holy Spirit from me. Restore the joy of Your salvation to me, and give me a willing spirit.

"How dare David pray to hear joy and gladness!" some might scream. Remember, David was a musician; he played the harp. From David's courage facing Goliath to his soothing songs in the presence of

King Saul, David was confident in his God. His sense of self-worth, his identity, and his courage all came from being a person consumed with God. Now, when he looked off his high balcony and saw a beautiful naked woman, he had long since fallen and was in need of repentance. John Phillips explains verse 8: "He had become deaf to the voice of God, deaf to all sounds of joy. Once he had been able to take his harp and make the halls of his palace ring with joy and gladness. No more! Now his inner agony was as great as the physical agony of broken bones. He had no way to restore the song to his soul, no way to get back the spiritual tenderness, which once made it possible for him to hear the voice of God. To know gladness and joy . . ."[7]

Restoration from sexual sin must go past the act to the source. People looking for satisfaction in what God has forbidden have ceased finding their satisfaction in Him. Turning from this sort of idolatry back to God is genuine, biblical repentance. Often God rebuked the Israelites for spiritual adultery, which in that day was often linked with sexual worship practices involving false gods. In Psalms 51, David repents of spiritual adultery as well as physical adultery. David desperately wanted God to be the center of his life once again. Similarly, the restoration of fellowship between God and His child requires a real change of direction where the offender begins to receive his joy, significance, and cleansing through his relationship with Jesus. In their book *Transformational Discipleship*, Geiger, Kelley, and Nation use David as the example of what they call *Offensive Discipleship*. They say of Psalms 51, "In verse 2 David uses the word guilt from the Hebrew word *avah*, which means 'twisted out of shape.' David is saying, 'God, the problem with my heart is that it was not centered on You.'"[8]

Remain Humble

So, the realization of sin and God's mercy followed by true repentance leads one down the path of restoration, which then ensues into worship. In the last of David's prayer, humility issues forth

---

[7] John Phillips, Exploring the Psalms Volume 1, (Grand Rapids, MI: Kregel, 1988) 407.
[8] Eric Geiger, Transformational Discipleship, (Nashville, TN: B&H Publishing Group and Lifeway Research, 2012) 37.

completing his journey to restoration. Verses 16–19 demonstrate why David had been effective as king in the past—his humility. He cried out:

> You do not want a sacrifice, or I would give it; You are not pleased with a burnt offering. The sacrifice pleasing to God is a broken spirit. God, You will not despise a broken and humbled heart. In Your good pleasure, cause Zion to prosper; build the walls of Jerusalem. Then You will delight in righteous sacrifices, whole burnt offerings; then bulls will be offered on Your altar (Psalms 51:16–19).

It is as though David was saying, "I want to remain humble so as to not miss worshipping You, God." These closing verses reveal that David understood God as the reason for the blessings upon the land, not the earthly king.

In addition, notice David's emphasis on worship in this psalm. As he depended on God to prosper the kingdom in spite of his mistakes, he recognized the prominent role of public worship, which follows private worship. Here is the problem with so many who claim to follow Christ today. They go to church, but they do not have a heart of worship. They lack the understanding, or at least fail in the application of the truth, that their bodies are the temple of the Holy Spirit. Others claim to worship God in their own way but eschew organized church. They have rejected the book of Acts; moreover, they have missed the point of the New Covenant, which is to make disciples of all nations and, in effect, bring them into the visible church or the fellowship of the saints for edification and maturation (see Matthew 28:18–20; Acts 2:38–47; and Ephesians 4). Today, people avoid what has historically been termed covenant church membership because they are often avoiding accountability. Insofar as one is outside the life of the local visible church, one is outside the will of God, and this is hazardous to one's spiritual well-being. For hope, healing, and restoration in the life of one who has fallen into sexual sin, the local church is indispensable.

So, where did all this leave David? At the end, David was in the center of God's will impacting his family for good. In amazing providence, God would one day send His Son, Jesus, through the lineage of David and his stolen bride, Bathsheba. David was a broken man, but he was a man satisfied with God alone. He was a man God described as loyal (1 Samuel 13:14). Over one thousand years later, the apostle Paul, preaching to the Jews in Antioch, restated this description and added, "From this man's descendants, according to the promise, God brought the Savior, Jesus, to Israel" (Acts 13:23).

Some might misconstrue the sovereignty of God in all of this and believe that David's sin did not matter, or that it was actually good. The Bible, however, teaches that God is not a mixture of light and darkness (1 John 1:5). God transcends time and space, and brings His plan to pass no matter what (Job 42:2). Paul's familiar words ring out at this point: "We know that all things work together for the good of those who love God: those who are called according to His purpose" (Romans 8:28).

Removal of the Curse

For the one involved in sexual immorality, there is hope only in Jesus. He forgave the woman caught in adultery and the woman at the well. He gave them life and peace. The same Gospel that lifts the original curse can lift the curse with which you have plagued your family. If your family members see in you the realization, repentance, restored worship, and humility epitomized in Psalms 51, they will be seeing God at work. Picture David on his deathbed talking to Solomon. David is able to give him the kingdom and point him in the right direction. A man or woman may decimate their family through sexual sin, just as David did, and God may punish or withhold blessings, but He will never leave nor forsake. Throughout the Gospel, God assures us, "I love you in spite of your sin." In Christ's blood, one can hear the Savior saying, "Turn your face away from their sins and blot out all their guilt. Create in them a clean heart for me and renew a steadfast spirit with them" (Psalms 51:9–10).

Remember, disingenuous apologies may demonstrate that one claiming to follow Christ is in fact unregenerate (not truly saved). Saul is a biblical example of this type of false repentance. He said, "I have sinned" (1 Samuel 27:21) just as David but without the path of brokenness. Judas Iscariot comes to mind as well when he said, "I have sinned" (Matthew 27:4a). Neither was restored.

Restoration comes not from simply admitting sin but from being disgusted with it and how you got there. Charles Swindoll says, "David died hating the day he fell into bed with Bathsheba because of the constant conflicts and consequences that resulted. But down inside he knew that the God of Israel had forgiven him and had dealt with him in grace."[9] Where are you? No matter how strong you may think you are, wisdom should lead you to remember David. He fell in an area of strength and during a season of blessing. Believers must also realize that the power of God's Spirit enables obedience. When we become overly dependent on our own strength, then sin finds expression even in areas of life that we deem to be fortified from failure.

If you have fallen into sexual sin and are genuinely seeking restoration, seek it the way David sought it. Many say time heals all wounds, but your sin should never start to look better or more tolerable to you. Jesus has healed you, not time. Distance helps only when there is true restoration. While there is freedom in the forgiveness, there is always the realization of the consequences of our sin and of what our salvation cost Him, namely His life. Keep the cross in mind when repenting of seemingly insignificant sins too. Because of Jesus and only because of Jesus, David would say, "Blessed is he whose transgression is forgiven whose sin is covered. Blessed is the man to whom the LORD does not impute iniquity and in whose spirit there is no deceit."[10]

QUESTIONS FOR REFLECTION

Personal Reflection

1. Is there any person or practice in your life that could be putting you in a similar situation with King David? In other words, are you where you are supposed to be and doing what God has called you to do?

2. Are you convicted by the Holy Spirit when you find yourself entertaining a lustful thought? If so, how do you respond to God? And, if not, why not?

3. Where is your walk with Jesus right now? As seen in our study of Psalms 51, David sought restored fellowship with God and

---

[9] Charles Swindoll, David, (Dallas, TX; Word Publishing, 1997) 207.
[10] Robert D. Bergen, The New American Commentary Volume 7 1, 2 Samuel, (Nashville, TN: Broadman & Holman Publishers, 1996) 386.

indicated that it was the key to joy and leading others to worship God. Is your daily quiet time inconsistent, stale, or both? What can you do to seek the Lord anew and afresh?

Group Reflection

1. What best practices to ensure a pure and guarded heart can we share with one another?

2. What can the church do to more faithfully present the Holy God of the Bible to believers and nonbelievers?

3. Discuss the New Testament idea of church discipline (see 1 Corinthians 5). What does loving, nonjudgmental accountability look like in the twenty-first century in the case of open sexual sin within the church membership?

Ashley E. Ray, DMin, has pastored four churches over the last seventeen years, including planting a church in Avon, Indiana, just west of Indianapolis. Called to preach the gospel at age fifteen and ordained at age nineteen, all under the ministry of Adrian Rogers, Ashley believes much has been given to him, and therefore much will be required of him. He sees preaching the Word in the context of the local church as his lifelong purpose. He holds degrees from Union University, Mid-America Baptist Theological Seminary, and The Southern Baptist Theological Seminary. He and his wife of fifteen years, Carrie, are blessed with a son, Harrison, and a daughter, Anna Grace. A native Memphian, Ashley and family came back to Memphis in 2009 where they serve Ridgeway Baptist Church. Ashley loves to spend time with his family and extended family as well as hunt and fish.

10

PARENTING A REBELLIOUS CHILD

INTRODUCTION

"It was the best of times; it was the worst of times." That famous opening line from Charles Dickens' masterpiece, *A Tale of Two Cities*, could easily be the subtitle of 2 Samuel. Inspired by God, the biblical author captured snapshots from the best of David's life but also snapshots of the worst. The first ten chapters chronicle the upwardly spiraling career of Israel's greatest king. His anointing as king of Judah, his ever-growing family, the reunification of the divided kingdom, his capture of and establishment of Jerusalem as his capital city, his covenant with God that established his enduring kingdom, and his successive victories over Israel's enemies all proved that David was blessed by God and the Lord was with him. Politically, militarily, spiritually, and domestically David had it all. It truly was the best of times.

Oftentimes, however, when a child of God is scaling the peak of a mountaintop experience with the Lord, Satan tempts the hardest, and that believer falls the farthest. Such was the case with David. From chapter 11 through the end of the book, the biblical author revealed David's "worst of times." In the eleventh chapter, with forthright transparency, the writer shined the spotlight on David's adulterous relationship with Bathsheba, his failed deceptive cover-up, and finally his murderous solution. What began in chapter 11 as a harmless rendezvous (at least in David's mind) with a beautiful woman became, in chapter 13, the fatal act that ushered rape, murder, and alienation into his family. Unknowingly, David had planted seeds of sin that, when fully grown, would blossom into death and rebellion, consequences he never envisioned. His "moment of indiscretion" actually became the impetus for his "worst of times."

It is highly unlikely when David's firstborn son, Amnon, came into the world, that David took the boy in his arms, looked deep into his eyes and said, "One day you will hatch a master plot to deceive me then rape your sister." David probably never imagined one son would rebel, much less two, but two indeed did. He had been a skilled shepherd, a loyal servant to King Saul, a mighty warrior, and an effective king, but he had no idea how to deal with two rebellious children.

Most dads never dream that one of their children will rebel against them. When God blesses a couple with a child, they rarely think the child will turn on them or God. Parents only think of lifelong family harmony and a child who will one day grow to be a faithful follower of Christ. Heartbreaking experiences have proven this utopian dream to be just that, a dream. Too many moms and dads have had to agonize over a wayward child, and they have no idea what to do. Just as road signs warn drivers where not to go, David's acts of ignorance and tentativeness warn dads where not to go in raising a rebellious child, but they also serve to pave a redemptive path to family wholeness.

TRIALS

"Now therefore, the sword will never leave your house because you despised Me and took the wife of Uriah the Hittite to be your own wife. This is what the LORD says, 'I am going to bring disaster on you from your own family: I will take your wives and give them to another before your very eyes, and he will sleep with them publicly'" (2 Samuel 12:10–11).

The stinging words of Nathan, the prophet, spoken in judgment on David's sin must have stunned the king. Uncontrolled urges and a sinful night of pleasure paved the way for years of heartache David never imagined while in the throes of passion. He had sinned, and even though God forgave him, consequences would come. Moreover, many of the consequences would come at the hands of his rebellious children.

The immediate consequence, and the only one not dealt through rebellious offspring, was the death of the child conceived with

Bathsheba. In 2 Samuel 12:14 Nathan said, "However, because you treated the LORD with such contempt in this matter, the son born to you will die." Verses 15 and 18 record the painful fulfillment of Nathan's prophecy: "The LORD struck the baby that Uriah's wife had borne to David, and he became ill . . . . On the seventh day the baby died."

Because David's sin was sexual, it is not surprising the second consequence would be sexual as well. David had several wives and numerous children by those wives. Second Samuel 13:1 introduces Absalom and the beautiful Tamar, siblings from the same mother, and Amnon, David's first son, born from a different mother. Amnon loved Tamar. However, his love was not the pure love of a brother, but rather the distorted love of a man who saw his sister as the means to satisfy his sensual appetite. He believed, however, that it would be impossible to fulfill his desires since Tamar was his half sister and the law prohibited such relationships. At the insistence of his cousin, Amnon conceived a plot that brought Tamar to his bedside. Feigning sickness, he asked David to send Tamar to care for him. When she arrived with food, Amnon "grabbed her and said, 'Come sleep with me, my sister'" (2 Samuel 13:11). When she refused, he raped her (2 Samuel 13:14). Having satisfied his base desires, he hated Tamar intensely and tossed her out of his house like worthless garbage. Second Samuel 13:21 says, "When King David heard about these things, he was furious." And no doubt he was broken.

David's third consequence spawned from the second. When Absalom learned Amnon had raped Tamar, he told his sister to remain quiet, just as he would do. Absalom hated Amnon and began planning revenge. Two years later, Absalom organized a great celebration for all his brothers and David as well. David declined the invitation so Absalom insisted that Amnon, the oldest son and heir-apparent to the throne, represent the king. Though suspicious, David agreed. Unbeknownst to the guests "Absalom commanded his young men . . . 'When I order you to strike Amnon, then kill him.' . . . So Absalom's young men did to Amnon just as Absalom had commanded" (2 Samuel 13:28–29). A plan of revenge, orchestrated by Absalom and two years in the making, played out perfectly but no doubt painfully for David. Second Samuel 13:37 states, "And David mourned for his son every day."[1]

---

[1] Most likely David was mourning for Amnon rather than Absalom who had fled in fear. See Bergen 386 in chapter 9.

The fourth consequence again came from the hand of Absalom. After Absalom lived five years in exile, David forgave him, brought him back to Jerusalem, and reconciled with him, or so he thought. Through a series of cunning events, Absalom won the hearts of the people and led a revolt against the king. So powerful was the revolt that David abandoned his throne and fled for his life with Absalom and his troops in pursuit (2 Samuel 15:14). The words of David in 2 Samuel 16:11 reveal the obvious pain he faced: "Then David said to Abishai and all his servants, 'Look, my own son, my own flesh and blood, intends to take my life.'"

The fifth consequence was a return to sexual sin. Because of David's adultery, Nathan said adultery would visit his home: "I will take your wives and give them to another before your very eyes, and he will sleep with them publicly" (2 Samuel 12:11). As Absalom was seeking to unify his power and rally the people of Israel in revolt, he sought the advice of Ahithophel, one of David's former advisors. Second Samuel 16:20, states, "Ahithophel replied to Absalom, 'Sleep with your father's concubines he left to take care of the palace. When all Israel hears that you have become repulsive to your father, everyone with you will be encouraged.' So they pitched a tent for Absalom on the roof, and he slept with his father's concubines in the sight of all Israel." True to the prophecy, David experienced the pain of infidelity and shame before the people. He had no one but himself to blame.

The final stinging consequence came as the troops of David and Absalom fought. David's troops prevailed and as Absalom was retreating from the battlefield, a tree limb lodged itself in his hair. As Absalom hung in midair, Joab thrust three spears into his heart killing him. When the news of Absalom's death came to David, he cried out, "My son Absalom! My son, my son Absalom! If only I had died instead of you, Absalom, my son, my son" (2 Samuel 18:33).

Shortly after David sinned with Bathsheba and murdered her husband Uriah, God said to him, "I am going to bring disaster on you from your own family." No doubt, David believed God, but it is unlikely he could foresee the pain to come. Looking back through painful years, he fully understood that forgiveness does not eliminate consequences and "whatever a man sows he will also reap" (Galatians 6:7).

TRUTH

The Bible's assessment of David is rather interesting and transparent. First Samuel 13:14 states that when God was looking for a replacement for King Saul he was seeking a "man loyal to Him." As the English Standard Version Bible states it, He was looking for "a man after His own heart." David was that man—loyal to God with a heart like the Father. He was not only loyal to God, but also to Saul. Chosen from tending his father's sheep, David became the personal attendant to Israel's king. He played the harp for him. He went to battle for him. He ate at his table as one of the king's own children. Even when Saul became jealous of David and tried to kill him, David remained loyal. In time, he proved himself a strong political leader. After Saul's death and David's ascension to the throne, he skillfully led a divided kingdom to unify, solidify, and thrive.

For all his successes, however, David was not perfect. With no hint of a cover-up, the Bible presents David with all of his warts. He lusted, committed adultery, deceived, murdered, and proved that while he could lead a nation, he could not lead a family. In many ways, David was incredibly wise, but when it came to his personal and family life, he ignored time-tested truths and paid dearly.

The first truth he ignored is that the actions and attitudes of parents have a tremendous influence on their children. The old adage "the apple doesn't fall far from the tree" is certainly true. No one is quite sure when and how this saying developed, but maybe it was born out of simple observation. Maybe Eve saw Cain and Abel acting like their dad and said, "the apple doesn't fall far from the tree." The simple truth is children take their cues from their parents. Children learn right and wrong from their parents. They learn how to act by watching their parents. While this truth is simple, yet biblical, David undoubtedly ignored it. His "apples" fell very close to the tree.

David's sin with Bathsheba was born out of lust. Second Samuel 11:2 states that one evening while David was strolling across the roof of the palace David saw a woman bathing in the adjoining courtyard. She was a beautiful woman and her beauty sparked desires within David that were not wholesome or holy. David had a wife. In fact, he had at least two wives at this point. He could have satisfied his longing within the bounds of marriage, but instead he looked, lusted, and took what he wanted. Verse 4 says, "David sent messengers to get her, and when she came to him, he slept with her."

Evidently, David was a man unable to conquer his lustful passion. This weakness became a model for Amnon. From his own dad he learned to see what you want and want what you see. Second Samuel 13:1–2 reveals that when Amnon saw Tamar, his sister, he saw she was beautiful, he was infatuated with her, he lusted for her, and he allowed the lust to take him to a sinful place. Verse 14 of the same chapter states that when Tamar refused Amnon's advances, "because he was stronger than she was, he raped her." He took what he wanted. The son had become like the father.

David's actions taught his son not only to act on lust, but also to lie. After Bathsheba discovered her night with David had led to pregnancy, David tried to cover up his sin. Uriah, Bathsheba's husband, was away from home on the battlefield. David concocted a plan that would bring Uriah home and allow him to spend time with his wife. As her body changed and the pregnancy became obvious, the natural conclusion would be that Uriah's leave of duty and time at home had produced the child. Rather than facing the music, David deceived.

Both Amnon and Absalom became master deceivers, just like their father. Amnon lied to David about being sick so the king would send Tamar to him, and Absalom organized the ambush of Amnon under the guise of a celebration. In a painful turn of events, David the deceiver was deceived by those who learned from his example.

David's actions also taught his son that the value of life is less than the value of personal satisfaction. When Uriah, out of respect for his fellow soldiers, refused to spend the evening with his wife, David's deceptive plan failed. Backed into a corner, David hatched a new plan, a plan that involved murder. He sent Uriah back to the battlefield with a message for Joab. David's instructions to his general were to place Uriah at the fiercest point of the battle, then have the troops back away. Without the support of his comrades, Uriah would no doubt perish. Uriah's death, which appeared to be a casualty of war, was actually murder. Once Uriah was out of the way, David could complete the cover-up and protect his integrity by marrying Bathsheba. The impression would be that the baby was David's, which it was, and it was born out of the marital relationship that began after David took Bathsheba as his wife. Uriah's life was of far less value to David than his personal pleasure and what others thought of him.

Absalom learned this lesson well from David. For two years, the desire for revenge grew in his heart, and for two years, he planned to satisfy that desire. Ironically, in the midst of revelry, Absalom took Amnon's life. Life, even his own brother's life, was of lesser value to him than murderous satisfaction.

The second truth David ignored was that passivity breeds more problems. On the battlefield, David was a man of action. On the throne, he was decisive. In his home, however, he was passive and inattentive. Second Samuel 13 reveals that Amnon's incestuous love for Tamar was obvious. Verse 2 says, "Amnon was frustrated to the point of making himself sick over his sister Tamar." So obvious was his disgraceful love that in verse 4 Jonadab asked, "Why are you, the king's son, so miserable every morning?" The fact that immediately following the rape, Absalom, in verse 20, assumed Amnon had raped Tamar is an indication that Amnon's love was obvious to all. No doubt David knew something was afoul, yet he did nothing. He remained silent. He did not confront Amnon, and furthermore, he sent Tamar to Amnon's home into an incident waiting to happen.

Not only was he passive with Amnon, but also with Absalom. David knew of the hatred between the two boys, yet he failed to address it. He, along with all of Israel, watched the bitterness seethe for two years. When Absalom requested Amnon's presence at the ambush masquerading as a celebration, David knew something was not right. He even asked Absalom, "Why should he go with you?" (2 Samuel 13:26). Instead of acting on what he saw and knew, David did nothing and the results were devastating. Had he acted, had he been assertive, it is very likely the rape and murder would have never occurred.

Even after Tamar's rape and Absalom's revolt, David did nothing. He brought no consequences upon Amnon or Absalom. His passivity subtly communicated that his children could do as they pleased without fear of consequences. By doing nothing, David's actions told Tamar she was unimportant to him and told Amnon and Absalom there were no consequences for their behavior.

The final truth David failed to believe is that while grace provides forgiveness, it does not eliminate consequences. David knew this. He had plenty of examples at which to look. God forgave Adam and Eve, but still expelled them from the Garden. God forgave Moses for murder, but the Egyptians still sought to kill him. God forgave Abraham for "helping" fulfill the promise of a child by impregnating

Hagar, but he still had to live with two jealous women and two sons at odds with one another.

Nathan confronted the sinful king and David confessed, "I have sinned against the Lord." To which Nathan replied, "The Lord has taken away your sin; you will not die" (2 Samuel 12:13). He experienced the grace of God. He should have died, but God forgave him and allowed him to live. However, consequences followed. Had he remembered this truth while peering at Bathsheba from the roof, he may very well have walked away from a beautiful woman and avoided a life of heartache.

The harsh reality is that David created the rebels who turned his home upside down. He brought the sin into his home, which led to rebellious behavior, and he failed to lead his family through the consequences of his sin. Scripture is clear in 2 Samuel 12:10–11 that David was culpable: "Now therefore, the sword will never leave your house because you despised Me and took the wife of Uriah the Hittite to be your own wife. This is what the LORD says, 'I am going to bring disaster on you from your own family: I will take your wives and give them to another before your very eyes, and he will sleep with them publicly.'" David had no one to blame but the one who looked back at him in the mirror.

In 1 Corinthians 10:6, speaking of Old Testament saints, Paul said, "Now these things became examples for us, so that we will not desire evil things as they did." Not all examples are positive, but all examples can teach. David made some terrible mistakes from which men can learn. His life is a case study in contrast: a man after God's own heart, but a man who ignored unalterable truths. Too often today, in our fast-paced world, men fail to make time to know God's unalterable truths. Without knowledge of God's Word, men inevitably fail. The failure of a dad often becomes the seeds of rebellion in and failure of his children. They see dad trying to "make it" disconnected from God's truth and assume that is how you do life. Sadly, many dads are passing along to their children a dangerous paradigm for life. Many dads are modeling that you can alter God's truth and get away with it unscathed. No one gets away with ignoring God's truth. Paul said, "Don't be deceived: God is not mocked. For whatever a man sows he will also reap" (Galatians 6:7). Men today must learn from David's failures that God's people do not define His truths, but rather His truths define His people.

TRANSFORMATION

Many men, just like David, have blown it personally and with their children. They have sinned before God, ushered the devastating consequences of sin into their families, and pushed their children, simply by their actions, to rebel against God and His truth. The good news is that God is a God of hope and second chances! Christianity is not a fatalistic religion but rather a redemptive relationship. God is in the business of redeeming humans and seemingly hopeless situations. David failed to act. The Bible's silence of any positive parenting steps David took to lead his family of rebels to wholeness speaks volumes. If you are a dad who has helped usher unhealthy lifestyles or rebellion into your home, learn from David's lack of action. Act now and allow God to stop the cycle and redeem the day.

Many men have never taken the first step to redeem their situation. It all begins with honesty before God. Restoration and healing begins when a man honestly and transparently tells God what He already knows: "For all have sinned and fall short of the glory of God" (Roman 3:23). The personal failures and parenting sins a man makes are just that, sin. First John 1:9 states what a sinner must do with sin and what God does with it in response: "If we confess our sins, He is faithful and righteous to forgive us our sins and to cleanse us from all unrighteousness." Sinners confess and God forgives! He removes the stain and penalty of sin. David knew this from personal experience. When Nathan confronted him, David confessed his sin. Expressing the grace of God, Nathan said, "The Lord has taken away your sin; you will not die" (2 Samuel 12:13). God forgave, and extended grace. Begin here, Dad. Confess your sins and He will forgive.

Oftentimes, because a stubborn man refuses to confess his sins, his heart becomes calloused, and he actually fails to recognize unconfessed sin.[2] Over time, he may forget his sins, but that does not absolve him of the responsibility to confess them. For real healing and restoration to begin a man may need to set aside extended time to pray through the events of his life, asking God to point out sin in his life or remind him of sin he has never confessed. Gregory Frizzell's book,

[2] See Leviticus 5:17.

Returning to Holiness: A Personal and Churchwide Journey to Revival, is a great resource to walk a man through a season of confession and cleansing.

Restoration begins when a man confesses his sin and God deepens it when a man assumes responsibility. Men are notorious for shifting the blame and failing to assume responsibility. The male penchant for such behavior goes all the way back to the Garden of Eden. After Adam and Eve sinned and the Lord confronted them, Adam said, "The woman You gave to be with me—she gave me some fruit from the tree, and I ate" (Genesis 3:12). In one breath, Adam shirked responsibility and blamed both Eve and God! It is as if he was saying, "It's not my fault. You are responsible because you gave me the woman, and she is responsible because she gave me the fruit."

Often, men want to blame everyone and everything for their bad decisions, sinful lifestyles, and poor parenting. It is true that many men grew up in a bad home environment where God was never mentioned, where sin was not only tolerated but celebrated, and a positive male role model never existed. Certainly, that produces a hole from which a man must work, but it does not provide an "out" from making good decisions, living a holy life, and parenting with love. When a man shirks responsibility and blames others, he loses the respect of his family. He becomes small in his wife's eyes and weak to his children. A man unwilling to own his past is inviting rebellion into his home. His children learn from him they can make bad decisions, blame someone else, and move on. Wholeness comes when a man accepts responsibility. He earns respect and teaches his children they too must shoulder their own decisions.

On a personal note, my grandmother was a loving woman who expressed love to her two children regularly. My grandfather, however, was just the opposite. If he loved his children, they did not know it because he did not know how to express love. He was a hard-working man who taught his sons how to work, but not how to love. It would have been easy for my dad to follow the only male example he had, unplug from the lives of his children, and blame it on his upbringing. Instead, he owned the situation, learned how to genuinely love, explained to me and my brother how he was raised, and expressed love to us daily. As I grew to be a teenager, I began to understand how my dad had "manned up" and assumed responsibility for his life. Consequently, my respect for him deepened and I learned a healthy pattern that has served me well in expressing love to my own wife and kids.

Closely related to assuming responsibility is sharing sin stories with family. David's sons grew up under the shadow of his sin. While David tried to keep his sin with Bathsheba a secret, it was impossible. Too many people knew. David's servants knew. Nathan knew. Joab knew. Consequently, his children grew up hearing whispers of his indiscretion. There is no record that David ever sat his children down and explained his sinful actions and the harsh consequences that ensued. David missed a teachable moment. If his sons had heard him explain the false allure of temptation, the guilt of sinfulness, and the pain of consequences, they may have steered clear of their own sinful choices.

I recently had a conversation with a godly young man in my church. He told me of a bad marital decision he made early in his life. The woman he married, a woman he should have never married, was unfaithful. The painful experience led to divorce. God has since brought him through a healing process, given him a wonderful, godly wife, and beautiful children. He ended the story by saying, "One day I will tell my children. They need to hear my story and they need to hear it from me. They need to learn from my mistakes so they will never make the same choices I made." That man has it right. He is paving the way to wholeness for his family and will be providing his children with insights that will hopefully prevent them from rebelling against God and their parents. Children may not need to know all the sordid details of sinful actions, but hearing a dad explain the consequences of his sin will go a long way in helping them avoid their own pitfalls.

Sometimes, even though parents push all the right buttons, express the right kind of love, and model the right kind of life, kids rebel. Then what? Love, that is what. Unconditional love. Luke makes it clear in Luke 15:1–3 that the parable of the prodigal son, along with the parable of the lost sheep and the parable of the lost coin, is about God's attitude when a lost sinner comes to Christ. However, through the parable, Jesus provides wonderful guidance for dealing with rebellious children. Above all, the father loved the prodigal. He did not approve of the sin. He did not allow the son to bring the sin into his home, but he never stopped loving him. He lovingly waited for the boy to return and when he did, the father showered him with love. He did not belittle the boy. He did not create unrealistic conditions the boy had to meet in order to live in the home. He simply welcomed him home with open arms of love.

Oftentimes when a child rebels, he or she is looking for love and acceptance, but in the wrong place. If a dad is trying to pave a path of reconciliation and wholeness, then he must pave it with the very thing the rebel is seeking—love! Revisiting Paul's description of love in 1 Corinthians 13 provides a good reminder to any dad of the kind of love his children need.

David's family story does not begin or end well. He sinned and brought trouble into his home. He ignored the early signs of rebellion and allowed the trouble to escalate. When the rebellion fully bloomed, he showed no aptitude or even desire to deal with it. In the end, all David had to show for it were the graves of two sons and a daughter who lived out the remainder of her life in disgrace. No dad should ever think that his situation must end like David's. God has made provision for both hope and healing.

QUESTIONS FOR DISCUSSION

Personal Reflection

1. Set aside some time alone to reflect upon your life. Are there sinful decisions or actions from your past or present that are negatively affecting your marriage and family? What action must you take regarding these sins in order to bring spiritual and family wholeness into your life?

2. As you think about the truths David ignored, which, if any, are you ignoring?

3. First Corinthians 16:14 says, "Your every action must be done with love." In light of Paul's description of love in 1 Corinthians 13, can you honestly say that your actions as the dad of either a rebellious or compliant child are demonstrated in love? If not, what steps are you going to take today?

Group Reflection

1. What do you think was David's biggest mistake in dealing with the rebellion in his home?

2. While there is no "cookie cutter" solution to dealing with rebellious children, what is a healthy outline for how dads should approach children with a wild streak?

3. What are some of the consequences evident today in our society due to passive dads?

4. What does loving a rebellious child look like? How can you support a family with a rebellious child or accept love and support for your rebellious child?

Michael Priest has been the senior pastor at Bartlett Baptist Church in Bartlett, Tennessee, since January of 2003. He earned a BA in biblical studies from Blue Mountain College, an MDiv in biblical studies from New Orleans Baptist Theological Seminary, and a PhD in Greek and New Testament from New Orleans Baptist Theological Seminary. Michael is married to Carolyn, his wife of twenty-eight years. They are blessed to have four sons: Jonathan, Caleb, David, and Matthew. He enjoys all sports, especially football, baseball, basketball, and hockey. He also loves the outdoors and rock climbs and mountaineers as often as possible.

11

FACING FAMILY PROBLEMS WITH PUBLIC SCRUTINY

INTRODUCTION

The advent of the information age with its Internet blogs and Facebook pages has opened a brave new world for those inclined to scrutinize and criticize. Twitter and Tumblr are newfound forums to better accomplish the age-old assault on the character of others. These venues have made public news that was once more private, and with greater publicity comes greater embarrassment to the victim. The follower of Christ must learn the appropriate response when confronted with the criticism hurled either from the lips or keyboard of a verbal assailant.

David experienced such a moment in his life in an otherwise obscure passage found in 2 Samuel 16:5–14. In a humiliated state, David fled Jerusalem and the threats of his rebellious son Absalom. While passing through the area of Bahurim (a city of the tribe of Benjamin), David encountered a relative of the former King Saul. Filled with resentment and bitterness, Shimei began to yell curses at David and his entourage, and not satisfied with what appeared to be a lack of response from the embattled king, threw stones and falsely accused David of murdering Saul.

To make matters worse, Shimei pointed to David's rebellious son as proof that God was displeased with the king. "Look you are in trouble because you're a murderer!" verse 8 says. With an already heavy spirit, David knew far more than this Benjamite of his guilt of murder and more. This man, whose heart raced toward God, lived in the same flesh as men today. And he, like those who have followed, fell far short of his goal of holiness. It is this self-guilt that often makes responding to false accusation more difficult.

One of King David's faithful lieutenants, his nephew named Abishai, offered to silence the annoying critic on David's behalf. "Then Abishai son of Zeruiah said to the king, 'Why should this dead dog curse my lord the king? Let me go over and cut his head off!'" (2 Samuel 16:9). This clear response of the flesh is met by the more spiritual response of the king. In words of restraint, David reminded his followers that there was a bigger picture to consider. Banishment from the palace by a malcontented son is a far greater concern than hearing insults hurled by an outsider. Further evidence of David's contrition is seen in the next verses. They suggest the possibility that what Shimei was doing was in the will of God.

A final and pivotal element of pain is caused by David's love for his rebellious son. As we saw in the last chapter, David's heart was heaviest because of the hatred he experienced from Absalom. David's faith in God and his spiritual response to this accuser helped validate his message of grace.

It is your inner circle that needs your response to public criticism to be spiritually mature. Having been a pastor for my entire adult life, I have endured my fair share of criticism. At times, my family has been sheltered from the harsh and sometimes unfair verbiage. But other times I needed my children to witness the right reaction to those challenges. It pleases me to know that neither of my adult sons developed a cynicism or disdain for the church as they have grown into adulthood. Your quiet response, like David before you, matters more than the garish voice of your opposition.

TRIALS

It would be a rare scenario that anyone could go through life without facing something akin to King David's experience in Bahurim. We occupy a fallen world with a very real enemy set to disrupt and destroy the testimony of the saints. We have been warned by Christ to expect opposition. In what would be some of His final words to the apostles, Jesus said:

> If the world hates you, understand that it hated Me before it hated you. If you were of the world, the world would love you as its own. However, because you are not of the world, but I have chosen you out of it, the world hates you. Remember the word I spoke to you: "A slave is not greater than his master." If they persecuted Me, they will also persecute you. If they kept My word, they will also keep yours. But they will do all these things to you on account of My name, because they don't know the One who sent Me. If I had not come and spoken to them, they would not have sin. Now they have no excuse for their sin. The one who hates Me also hates My Father. If I had not done the works among them that no one else has done, they would not have sin. Now they have seen and hated both Me and My Father. But this happened so that the statement written in their scripture might be fulfilled: They hated Me for no reason (John 15:18–25).

Unlike David, Jesus never sinned. And if Jesus, who was without sin, was criticized, how much more might those who are imperfect expect to receive? It is the believer's response to the public criticism that indicates the depth of his relationship to God. The encounter with Shimei, for example, showed a different David than the one who had failed God previously. The contrition that followed his adultery with Bathsheba, the murder of her husband Uriah, and the confrontation with Nathan, led David to a place of repentance. Tests like the one in Bahurim provided the king an opportunity to prove that God was at work in his life.

Tests are designed for that purpose. David declared in verse 10: "He curses me this way because the Lord told him, 'Curse David.'" This gives us better perspective. The king looked past the insults of a mad man in order to see the sovereign activity of God. We are told in James 1:2–4, "Consider it a great joy, my brothers, whenever you experience various trials, knowing that the testing of your faith produces endurance. But endurance must do its complete work, so that you may be mature and complete, lacking nothing." The king passed the test and by so doing illustrated for every man in every generation an example of how to overcome evil with good.

So how did David do it? How might men today be expected to see the trials and public scrutiny of life as blessings of opportunity rather than hurtful annoyances? First, David accepted the cursing if not the charge. He was purely innocent of the blood of Saul as he was being accused, but the same conscience that cleared him of that allegation may very well have reminded him of the innocent blood of Uriah of which he was guilty. "A humble tender spirit will turn reproaches into reproofs, and so get good by them, instead of being provoked by them."[1]

Second, David kept the focus on the bigger picture. David's response to Abishai gives us insight on how we are expected to respond to critics: "Sons of Zeruiah, do we agree on anything?" (2 Samuel 16:10a). These two men were on the journey together headed toward the same destination. The challenge at Bahurim simply proved they were not focused on the same thing. David represented the better focus. David saw the kingdom hanging in the balance while Abishai saw only the annoyance. Your focus will help determine your response.

A turning point in the Revolutionary War occurred on a cold, blustery winter's evening. "It was a demoralized, ill-equipped army which stood on the shore of the Delaware River in December of 1776 . . . The year had not gone well for the army. Washington's men had suffered horrendous defeats in New York at the hands of British and Hessian soldiers. The losses of Forts Washington and Lee had levied a heavy toll to the Patriot cause as many troops were killed or taken prisoner, much needed supplies/munitions were abandoned in the evacuation of the forts, and the belief in the possible achievement of independence was dwindling at every turn."[2] But then, General George Washington devised a plan for crossing the river and surprising the Hessian Army at Trenton. He and Lieutenant Colonel John Cadwalader and General James Ewing were to cross the Delaware in the dark and make the assault the next morning. When dawn approached, only Washington and his men stood on the east bank of the Delaware. History reports that Cadwalader and Ewing were unsuccessful in crossing the river. "Cadwalader turned back because he was unable to get his artillery across and Ewing abandoned the plan entirely."[3] These two saw the obstacles while General Washington seized the opportunity. The

---

[1] Matthew Henry, Matthew Henry's Commentary on the Whole Bible: Complete and Unabridged in One Volume "2 Samuel 16:5–14," (Peabody: Hendrickson, 1994).
[2] "Washington's Crossing," Pennsylvania Historical and Museum Commission, http://www.ushistory.org/washingtoncrossing/history/crossing.htm
[3] Ibid.

former we know little of, the latter continues to be celebrated more than two hundred years after his death.

What you focus on when public scrutiny and criticism are hurled in your direction will determine how you will be remembered by those you influence. With your eyes fixed firmly on eternal matters, you may be able to accomplish more during a moment of adversity than in a lifetime of prosperity. The goal of every follower of Christ is to live in such a way that Jesus is glorified in your life. That focus helps to keep the proper perspective in times of distress, and it is that focus that will communicate to your associates the depth of your faith in God.

TRUTH

The confrontation at Bahurim illustrates the fact that no one is exempt from family problems and public scrutiny. If the king of Israel at the height of national prosperity can be pushed aside by a power-hungry son and mocked by a village commoner, then any of us might expect some of the same treatment (see 2 Samuel 16:6). Keep in mind that times of rebellion can also be times of revelation. These moments help us see people as they really are. It is the last spoken words of David in this narrative that provide us the truth to which we should cling: "Perhaps the Lord will see my affliction and restore goodness to me instead of Shimei's curses today" (2 Samuel 16:12).

David knew full well both the grace of God and the authority of God. Embracing these two realities can be very liberating to even the weakest of saints. Just as Satan, the enemy of God, was behind the taunts and insults hurled at the king, the Spirit of God was at work in the heart and soul of David, reminding him of the eventual victory that was his and could not be aborted. The Bible says, "So David and his men continued along the road while Shimei was going along the hillside opposite him, cursing as he went and throwing stones at him and showering him with dirt. The king and all the people with him arrived at their destination exhausted. And there he refreshed himself" (2 Samuel 16:13–14). David and his entourage continued on their journey, finally reaching their destination. The promise of God is that you will reach your destination. The rock throwing and insult hurling may continue for a season, but God's eternal plan for you cannot be aborted (see John 42:2).

The variable in this is the impact that you will have on those closest to you. It has been well established that you are a trophy of grace. Guilty, yet pronounced innocent, and challenged to stand on the promises of God or gravitate to the natural inclinations of the flesh and fight back. To hear the insults, justified or not, to glean any helpful nugget contained within, and then to let the rest slide off you like the second scoop of a vanilla cone on a hot July afternoon, proves 1 John 4:4: "But you belong to God, my dear children. You have already won a victory over those people, because the Spirit who lives in you is greater than the spirit who lives in the world" (NLT). A spiritual response opens the door to evangelism with those who know you best. There are a number of other lessons that can be discovered from David's encounter with Shimei that will be useful to you as you continue on your journey toward life's destination.

First, you can expect the unexpected. Years had passed since the death of Saul and the ascension of David to the throne, thus making the insults and accusations that bombarded him that day very old news. It is not unreasonable to assume that he was surprised that Shimei was just now attacking. Why the delay? The misfortune of Absalom's uprising had put David in a vulnerable state. The enemy looks for windows of opportunity to pounce on the child of God, and when he is beaten down by circumstances, he is most vulnerable. Family problems, for example, are a quick trigger to overwhelm even the most faithful among us.

Second, we must admit that even the most idealized can disappoint. It can be crushing to discover that a person we admire has faults and imperfections. The biblical record of David's life is an ironic twist that offers hope to us all. If a man of his stature is capable of sin and cover-up, then anyone is. And if someone guilty of adultery and murder can be restored, then anyone can. "No temptation has overtaken you except what is common to humanity. God is faithful, and He will not allow you to be tempted beyond what you are able, but with the temptation He will also provide a way of escape so that you are able to bear it" (1 Corinthians 10:13). We find the power to bear the public scrutiny and harsh judgments because Jesus bore them for us.

Finally, we must remember that He will get us through. "Today, our Lord Jesus is despised and rejected of men, just as David was during the rebellion. It takes courage for men and women today to remain loyal to the King, but we can be sure that God will reward such loyalty when Jesus returns."[4] God has both the power and the prerogative to bring you through the most difficult of times. Disease, death, and divorce are but a few of the opportunities the enemy uses to weaken the resolve of the faithful. Remember when Satan attacked Job? The primary intent of the devil was to prove Job's devotion to God was based on the blessings he enjoyed and not on his authentic fear of God. Satan believed that he could expose and defeat Job if his life was disrupted. The loss of possessions, family, and even his health did not deter the righteous one. Satan said, ". . . . A man will give up everything he owns in exchange for his life. But stretch out Your hand and strike his flesh and bones, and he will surely curse You to Your face" (Job 2:4–5).

With the act done, and in his agony, Job responded to his wife's advice to "curse God and die" by saying, "You speak as a foolish woman speaks, should we accept only good from God and not adversity?" And the Bible records, "Throughout all this Job did not sin in what he said" (Job 2:4–10).

TRANSFORMATION

The patience and restraint of King David on this occasion was amazingly different from his violent reaction to the insults aimed at him earlier in his life. On the earlier occasion, the Bible says:

> While David was in the wilderness, he heard that Nabal was shearing sheep, so David sent 10 young men instructing them, "Go up to Carmel, and when you come to Nabal, greet him in my name." Then say this: "Long life to you, and peace to you, to your family, and to all that is yours. I hear that you are shearing. When your shepherds were with us, we did not harass them, and nothing of theirs was missing the whole time they were in Carmel. Ask your young men, and they will tell you. So let my young men find favor with you, for we have come on a feast day. Please give whatever you can afford to your servants and to your

[4] W. W. Wiersbe, Wiersbe's Expository Outlines on the Old Testament "2 Samuel 15:13–16:23," (Wheaton, IL: Victor Books, 1993).

> son David." David's young men went and said all these things to Nabal on David's behalf, and they waited. Nabal asked them, "Who is David? Who is Jesse's son? Many slaves these days are running away from their masters. Am I supposed to take my bread, my water, and my meat that I butchered for my shearers and give them to these men? I don't know where they are from." David's men retraced their steps. When they returned to him, they reported all these words. He said to his men, "All of you, put on your swords!" So David and all his men put on their swords. About 400 men followed David while 200 stayed with the supplies (1 Samuel 25:4–13).

The younger, less contrite David was restrained not by his own conscience but by the swift and courteous action of a beautiful and intelligent woman named Abigail. The Scripture goes on to tell us that she intercepted David and his men on their way to kill Nabal. Intervening on his behalf, she offered supplies to the young warrior. David was pleased and said to her; "Praise to the Lord God of Israel, who sent you to meet me today! Blessed is your discernment, and blessed are you. Today you kept me from participating in bloodshed and avenging myself by my own hand" (1 Samuel 25:32–33). The transformation in David's life is made clear by these two contrasting responses.

To further illustrate this transformation, King David himself penned the words to Psalms 3 as he fled from Jerusalem and his son Absalom. These words may very well have been written as he rested from the journey through Bahurim.

> Lord, how my foes increase! There are many who attack me. Many say about me, "There is no help for him in God." But You, Lord, are a shield around me, my glory, and the One who lifts up my head. I cry aloud to the Lord, and He answers me from His holy mountain. I lie down and sleep; I wake again because the Lord sustains me. I am not afraid of the thousands of people who have taken their stand against me on every side. Rise up, Lord!
> Save me, my God! You strike all my enemies on the cheek; You break the teeth of the wicked. Salvation belongs to the Lord; may Your blessing be on Your people (Psalms 3).

As is often the case in our life's journey, we need the prompting of God's Spirit to help us maintain or regain the proper perspective in times of distress. One sure way to keep balance is found by reading the psalms. Whatever mood or emotion we may be experiencing, there is a psalm related to it that speaks both to God and to our own hearts. It offers Him what we wish to say but in an emotional moment find words hard to come by. In addition, it brings comfort to our soul by reminding us of the power and grace of the Almighty. Psalms 3 is such a psalm. In it, we find the secret to living in victory when we feel like giving up.

First, we must embrace the personal approach that David enjoyed with God. "Lord . . ." he begins. The Hebrew word is *Jehovah* and it is considered the Israelites' supreme name for God. The Hebrews would later hold it in such high regard that they refused to say it aloud. Here, however, is the disgraced king coming boldly to the throne room of the Almighty. Not satisfied to speak *of* God, David insisted on speaking *to* Him. This same confidence can be enjoyed by every follower of Christ. The Bible says, "Therefore let us approach the throne of grace with boldness, so that we may receive mercy and find grace to help us at the proper time" (Hebrew 4:16). This was indeed a proper time for David to receive mercy and find grace to help. In similar moments, you will find Him just as personal and available to extend to you that same divine grace and mercy.

Second, we notice that David is neither naïve nor sheltered from the harsh reality life offers. His words in verse 1, ". . . how my foes increase!" open the window into his troubled soul. As is often the case, the mob mentality reigns in circumstances like this one. As the attackers multiply, supporters disappear. And as the number of critics grows, so too does the cruelty of their comments, arriving at the crescendo of suggesting that even God would not be willing to help this time.

A child of God is never more hopeless than when he is convinced there is no help for him in God. Maybe you have felt what the despised monarch was feeling that day. The very real and recognized circumstances of verses 1 and 2 must quickly be negated by the hope existing in one's relationship with the Divine and confessed in the remaining portion of the psalm. We must take a personal approach with God even as we acknowledge the definite and deliberate assault from the enemy.

The third and most important step in living victoriously while being publically assailed comes in the next two verses. A declaration of rock-solid faith in God is never more necessary than in these times of distress. "But You, Lord, are a shield around me, my glory, and the One who lifts up my head. I cry aloud to the Lord, and He answers me from His holy mountain" (Psalms 3:3–4). The Hebrew word for "shield" in this verse is *magen* and is the same word spoken centuries before by God Himself in reference to how He would protect Abram as he pursued the Lord's will (see Genesis 15:1). The principle does not change. In a moment not unlike David's, and in answer to the question, "Why don't you publically respond and turn on the lights to what is going on behind the scenes?" then President Jerry Rankin of the International Mission Board of the Southern Baptist Convention replied, "Ed (Stetzer), I don't need to. God brings what they do to light, and every time it hurts them and not us."[5] As Dr. Rankin reminds us, it is always in our best interest to trust God as our shield. He secures us on all sides. The apostle Paul stood on the same promise in Romans 8:31 when he said, "What then are we to say about these things? If God is for us, who is against us?"

In addition to confessing that God is his shield, David refers to Him as "his glory." This intriguing assertion causes quite an ironic twist to the scene. David was disgraced and his crown scorned. As he retains no splendor of his own, God and His glory continue to radiate through him! What was not the best days *for* King David may have been the best days *of* King David.

God is his shield, his glory, and "the lifter of his head." This picturesque illustration shows how a dejected king responds in faith. With his spirit sinking and his head drooping, David proclaimed his dependence on God to restore his joy and to lift his head. Psalms 30 is the testimony that his faith in God to bring back his joy had been fulfilled!

I have kept a journal through the years (sometimes more faithfully than at others) describing the events and emotions that mark ministry. Remembering one of the difficult times and wanting to refer to it in a sermon, I leafed through the pages during the coinciding days in hopes of recalling the exact details. As I sat on the floor, journals on either side, my wife lying on the bed hoping for an afternoon nap, I chuckled at what had been written several years prior. "Let me read you

---

[5] Ed Stetzer, "3 Things I Learned from Jerry Rankin," Between the Times, http://betweenthetimes.com/index.php/2013/09/24/things-i-learned-from-jerry-rankin/

this," I said, interrupting her solace. I read the circumstances and then this sentence, "I cannot imagine the pain of this day ever being equaled." She laughed out loud as we recalled how often the pain of that day had been surpassed. But it was the next sentence that made our hearts leap forward. I had written on that same occasion, "Today we cry but I am sure one day we will look back on this and laugh!" And that we did! And you might too.

David's final declaration of faith is seen in the third psalm, verse 4, "I cry aloud to the Lord, and He answers me from His holy mountain." Even though David was running further and further away from the mountain of God, he clung with confidence to the fact that His Lord would not turn a deaf ear to his circumstance. You may sometimes feel that God is in one place and you in another. In order to be strong in the face of accusation and innuendo, the child of God must be confident in his ability to call on God in prayer and be heard.

Your faith during troubling times should mirror that of King David. Remember, God is your shield and defender. He alone is your glory in moments of disgrace. He is able to lift your head from its position of humiliation, and when you pray, He will hear and answer according to His providence. This pattern of praise, peace, and prayer in the face of public pressure can sustain the child of God even in his most difficult hour. The enemy would like for you to focus on your plight, but reading the psalms helps you to refocus on God and your relationship that cannot be severed.

The final verses of Psalms 3 affirm the value of this formula. "I lie down and sleep; I wake again because the Lord sustains me" (Psalms 3:5). His flight from the palace and the threat of his son Absalom would have naturally created enough anxiety to interrupt David's rest. In addition, he knew the hunted must never fall into deep sleep for fear the hunter sneak up on him in his slumber. But his confidence in God served as the antidote to this despondency and remarkably provided both rest and protection. He was able to sleep and to sleep with the confidence that he would again awake.

Most of us assume that we will never see the level of public humiliation that King David faced in the days of Absalom's uprising. We are, however, living in an increasingly hostile world to those who follow Christ and must not assume total exemption from such an event. The "Shimei" in your life is far more likely to peck out letters on a keyboard than to pick up rocks from the roadside, but the pain from the experience is nonetheless real. This reality warrants careful attention to walking in tandem with God. Isaiah the prophet reminds us, ". . . but those who trust in the Lord will renew their strength; they will soar on wings like eagles; they will run and not grow weary; they will walk and not faint" (Isaiah 40:31). May this be true of you, even as the rocks fly!

QUESTIONS FOR DISCUSSION

Personal Reflection

1. In what ways can you relate to the insults and criticism David received from Shimei the son of Gera? Name a specific example.

2. Did your response reflect David's or Abishai's? Which has more value and why?

3. How did your response impact your family and close associates?

4. How can reading the psalms help you refocus and regain perspective while facing public scrutiny and criticism?

Group Reflection

1. How might you help someone facing public criticism and humiliation?

2. What can you do to prepare in the likelihood that you become the target of another's harsh critique?

3. How is replying to condescending emails and blogs with emails and blogs counterproductive?

Dr. Greg McFadden has served in the office of pastor since 1984. He came to the First Baptist Church of Humboldt, Tennessee, in 2002. He is a graduate of Union University and holds postgraduate degrees from Southern Baptist Theological Seminary and Luther Rice Seminary. He and his wife, Sheila, have three children: Ryan, Joey, and Lily. Greg loves to fish and continues his pursuit of the elusive ten-pound bass!

EDITOR'S NOTE

The formatting for the previous eleven chapters has been consistent. This template for the chapters was chosen for two primary purposes. The first was to expose how biblical truth speaks to real-life situations and by doing so help equip readers to apply the biblical truths to their lives and families. Secondly, the template was built upon specific events that occurred in David's life. Since specific life events were the foundation, then the Trials, Truth, and Transformation outline helped organize our analysis of the events and apply biblical truth. Chapter Twelve has a different format and focus. It is not built around a single event or life situation. Chapter Twelve is focused on David's desire for worship as expressed through his psalms. Therefore, the organization of the chapter is different. There is much for us to learn from David who was a "man after God's own heart" as we explore his heart for worship. Hopefully you will be encouraged, inspired, and motivated to be a more faithful and active worshipper as you engage with the truths outlined in this chapter.

12

EMBRACING GOD'S DESIRE FOR WORSHIP

INTRODUCTION

When a man worships, it not only changes his life but the lives of everyone around him.

David is a brilliant example of this. He first bursts onto the scene by his opposition to the giant Goliath, and all because he cannot stand Goliath's unworshipful slur against God (1 Samuel 17). Worship of God compels David to fight for the honor of God's great name. It is when David worships before the Lord, as he brings the ark into Jerusalem, that the true character of his wife and Saul's daughter, Michal, is revealed (2 Samuel 6). And it is worship that stops the plague God has sent on Israel after David's sin of numbering the people (2 Samuel 24).

Worship has just as powerful an influence in lives today as it did in David's. It is your worship that will change you and the lives of your family, friends, and coworkers. It will be the thing that empowers your witness, which separates you from those who do not truly worship, and that restores you to relationship with God when things get rocky because of your disobedience.

There are no more pertinent examples of David's worship and how it sprang from his relational connection to God than the psalms he authored. Here is a look at three such psalms of David—Psalms 18, 19, 24—and how they should shape and inform worship.

PSALMS 18 AND THE POWER OF WORSHIP

David has a special worship song for the choir director, the superscription of Psalms 18 tells us. It is a psalm he created and spoke personally to God the very day God delivered him from all his enemies, including Saul, the king of Israel. He describes himself as the servant of the Lord. By doing so, he acknowledges that he has been called by God to fulfill an important function among his people.

His function is to be a shepherd to his people, guiding them to true worship of God and offering his sword to protect his people and to execute justice in the land.

Though it is not made clear exactly when this praise song was written, it may be supposed that it was after Saul had died in battle and those who might have been opposed to David's kingship had finally acknowledged him as king (see 2 Samuel 1–5). And so, in the opening lines of this psalm, David lets it all hang out. In words that may feel uncomfortable to some men today, David begins by telling God that he loves Him.

Worship Means Love

Verse 1: "I love You, Lord, my strength."

When a man "worships" a woman, he has no problem telling her he loves her. But in American culture at least, it is often difficult for men to say to significant people—their children, their parents, their friends, and even God—that they love them. But this is very much the heart of worship. If you can't express your emotions, you cannot worship.

Do not stumble here. You may try to tell yourself that you worship God just fine with your mind and with your service, but Moses gave us God's command to love Him with all our hearts (Deuteronomy 6:4). And here David is doing just that. He is the man after God's own heart.

Why is it that men struggle so much here and David did not seem to? It is in part because in our culture we believe emotional expression makes us look weak. The epitome of weakness is seemingly a man crying. But the manliest of men in Scripture cry openly and unhesitatingly. Jesus (John 11:35), Peter (Luke 22:62), and Paul (Acts 20:36–38)—they know nothing of such nonsense.

God made us emotional because He is emotional, and He wants to relate with us on that level (Genesis 1:27; Deuteronomy 6:4). So the beginning of worship for any man or woman is connecting with the feelings we have for God.

Have you explored your feelings for God? What if you were to write down in a private journal the ways you feel toward God? Here's a rule of thumb: if you use the word "that" as in "I feel that . . ." you are likely not expressing a feeling. It might be helpful to go online and Google feeling words to give yourself some vocabulary. Love must express itself and true worship is made up of such expression.

Worship Gives Reasons for One's Love

David follows his expression of love for God with the reasons he loves Him.

Verses 2–3: "The Lord is my rock, my fortress, and my deliverer, my God, my mountain where I seek refuge, my shield and the horn of my salvation, my stronghold. I called to the Lord, who is worthy of praise, and I was saved from my enemies."

David has found God to be his place of security and protection, someone he can go to when he needs refuge. What are your reasons for loving God? Has He given you a job with which you can provide for your family, a wife and kids who love you, a church home that nestles you under its wings, or an ability to enjoy His good gifts in life? Then tell Him so! Tell Him how He has blessed you.

Have you ever noticed how your son, daughter, wife, or coworkers light up when you take the time to give them a thoughtful description of how wonderful they are? Haven't you experienced being given value by someone who expressed it in words? How did it make you feel? Of course you had to somewhat deflect it, make excuses for why all the credit shouldn't go to you, but it felt good inside, didn't it?

Well, believe it or not, God likes that too. He is very secure in who He is, but you still might say that He thrives on praise (Psalms 149:3–4). This psalm actually says that God delights in His people, which suggests that He desires praise from us and takes joy in it because He takes joy in us. When He sees us acknowledging Him as the most virtuous One, He is seeing us give priority to what is good, and that pleases Him.

Many have given testimony to the first time they saw Yosemite, Yellowstone, or some other amazing feature of God's creation. It took their breath away. If you were with your son or daughter and instead of marveling in Yosemite's El Capitan, one of the most stunning rock formations in the world, he or she could only focus on how hot or hungry he or she was, you would likely be disappointed with them. You would see this as a flaw in their character, a self-centeredness that did not bode well for the future. Even so, when we are so locked up in ourselves that we cannot give reasons for why we love God, we show great weakness of character.

In your private journal, consider listing the reasons God has given you to worship Him. Feel free to come back to those over and over as needed. It is good to be consumed with the glory of the greatest Being in the universe.

Worship Is Enhanced by Personal Righteousness

Verse 20: "The Lord rewarded me according to my righteousness; He repaid me according to the cleanness of my hands."

It has already been noticed that giving God worship means a person's priorities have been rightly ordered. David's own testimony in this psalm was that God gave him protection as a reward for his righteousness. David's priorities were rightly ordered, so much so, that when it came time to give credit for his own deliverance from death, he didn't praise himself; he praised God.

Are you so caught up in yourself that you actually believe that you're the cause for all the good things happening in your life? A fellow racquetball player is always quick to share an opportunity he had to help someone spiritually and yet never finishes his testimony without giving credit to God. "It's not me," he always says, "but God."

The heart that is right most naturally gives worship to the One who is behind all good things in life. Do you see what an impact this might have on those around you? Your wife would realize she could trust a husband who is not stuck on himself, but who acknowledges the true and living God. A son or daughter will respect a dad who honors God. They will learn that they too can become like Dad because it doesn't depend on how wonderful they are but on how wonderful God is. A coworker can see the humility that resides in you and grow to trust you in all matters, maybe even eternal matters.

True worship does not spring out of disobedience but out of a heart that is seeking to honor God and that sees every other priority as deficient. True worship thrives on personal righteousness. This in no way implies that if we are lacking in righteousness we cannot worship God. But if there is no desire to overcome unrighteousness, if we are content in our unrighteousness, worship will be a mere formality, not something pouring out from a heart full of gratitude and yearning for holiness.

Worship Empowers You

Verses 28–29: "Lord, You light my lamp; my God illuminates my darkness. With You I can attack a barrier, and with my God I can leap over a wall."

David experienced tremendous energy from his worship of God. It was like he was the oil in the lamp, and God was the fire that made him burn. It gave light to everything around him. With that kind of clarity and illumination, David could do anything. He could certainly defeat his enemies.

So can you. When you worship God with all your heart, you are developing confidence in the most powerful and most loving Being in the universe. You are coming in line with His truest purpose for you. You are feeding your faith spiritual Wheaties. Like Popeye downing a can of spinach, you are steeling your spiritual muscles for a victory.

Where are you struggling in your life right now? When David was facing his most dire circumstances, he worshipped. He didn't always feel empowered right away (ever notice how often he said, "How long, O God, how long?"). But turning his heart to God was the genius of his life. It served him well. It made him one of the most powerful men in the world, not a power demonstrated in muscle or might, but a power demonstrated in a peaceful and a brave heart.

Try this experiment. Focus on an area of your life that you are not happy about, one that is kicking your tail, so to speak. Then turn to the Lord and begin to worship Him, thanking Him for what He is doing through this situation in your life, explaining to Him where you see His hand at work, and even begging Him to show Himself more clearly in your circumstances. Then tell Him that no matter what He sends your way you are going to trust that He is bigger and badder than any circumstance you could face. Give Him praise for His power and purpose in your life. Open your heart to listen to what He might have to say back. Make any notes in your journal that are worth coming back to as a reminder.

Worship Is the True Source of All Victory

David finishes his song with a victory declaration:

> The Lord lives—may my rock be praised! The God of my salvation is exalted. God—He gives me vengeance and subdues peoples under me. He frees me from my enemies. You exalt me above my adversaries; You rescue me from violent men. Therefore I will praise You, Yahweh, among the nations; I will sing about Your name. He gives great victories to His king; He shows loyalty to His anointed, to David and his descendants forever (Psalms 18:46–50).

Psalms 18 is an amazing testimony to the power of worship in a man's life.

PSALMS 19 AND THE TRANSFORMING PRODUCTIVENESS OF WORSHIP

> The heavens declare the glory of God, and the sky proclaims the work of His hands. Day after day they pour out speech; night after night they communicate knowledge. There is no speech; there are no words; their voice is not heard. Their message has gone out to all the earth, and their words to the ends of the world. In the heavens He has pitched a tent for the sun. It is like a groom coming from the bridal chamber; it rejoices like an athlete running a course. It rises from one end of the heavens and circles to their other end; nothing is hidden from its heat. The instruction of the Lord is perfect, renewing one's life; the testimony of the Lord is trustworthy, making the

> inexperienced wise. The precepts of the Lord are right, making the heart glad; the command of the Lord is radiant, making the eyes light up. The fear of the Lord is pure, enduring forever; the ordinances of the Lord are reliable and altogether righteous. They are more desirable than gold—than an abundance of pure gold; and sweeter than honey, which comes from the honeycomb. In addition, Your servant is warned by them; there is great reward in keeping them. Who perceives his unintentional sins? Cleanse me from my hidden faults. Moreover, keep Your servant from willful sins; do not let them rule over me. Then I will be innocent and cleansed from blatant rebellion. May the words of my mouth and the meditation of my heart be acceptable to You, Lord, my rock and my Redeemer.

Psalms 19 allows us to realize the reason David wants to be cleansed from his hidden faults and kept from willful sin is so he can be acceptable to the God whose worth is made known through what He created and through what He has taught us in His law. This psalm is one of David's greatest. It is a marvelous hymn to the clarity of God's voice in creation and Scripture. Every day the sun, the moon, and the stars give testimony to God's greatness. No one can escape from hearing the witness he bears to who God is. Not everyone has the witness of Scripture, the law of the Lord, so these creation attestations of God's glory leave all without excuse when it comes to knowing Who is in charge of this world (see Romans 1:18–26).

God's law is even clearer in reference to what the human heart needs: renewal, wisdom, gladness, and light. Obeying this law brings purity, reliability, and righteousness. There is no more valuable gift God could give us.

This psalm is not just a way of telling the world how wonderfully God has borne witness to Himself. David is revealing his own heart here. He knows that he has motives that even he is not aware of at first until they express themselves in disobedience and rebellion. He is certainly aware that he is prone to out and out willful sin, and desires to be kept from it.

Such sinfulness leaves one defeated and controlled in ways that steal the renewal, wisdom, gladness, and light from one's life, and so he asks God not to let them rule over him. In a very real way, this is worship. Worship is recognizing your own failure and God's great goodness. It is seeking to bring your heart into conformity to God's character. It is recognizing that He alone can accomplish that.

Worship is a yearning to be acceptable to God. Such a yearning should not be out of terrifying fear that God is going to punish you, though certainly there is a justice in God that will not ever overlook the poisonousness of sin. This yearning most appropriately comes from the realization that God loves you and that such love will not tolerate anything less than the very best for you.

When you see wrong behavior or wrong attitudes in your children, you anticipate how such behaviors and attitudes will hurt them now and in the future. Your soul is stirred to correct these course deviations from the good life. You know that if you don't act, your child might grow to think that the world should bow at his or her feet. You know that such attitudes will have disastrous effects on those around them and that they will end up being alienated from the love and support they need in life. You cannot tolerate anything less than God's very best for them.

However, until your child worships God in such a way that he yearns to be acceptable to God, all his behaviors will be done more out of fear of consequences than out of a heart that is for God. Without that worshipful yearning to be acceptable to God, his righteousness will be the kind that is in it for what he can get out of it. It will not be the kind of righteousness that goes the extra mile because it is righteousness for righteousness' sake. It is goodness for goodness' sake. So "be good for goodness' sake" and not just because you want the rewards you think come from doing right.

Invite God to expose and cleanse you from hidden sins. Invite Him to keep you from blatant sin. Pay attention to the thoughts He places in your mind, and write them in your worship journal. It may seem like a scary thing to open yourself up to God's probing vision. But hey, He loves you. He's not concerned to show you the bad motives, thoughts, and behaviors you have so He can slam you. He wants to chisel you into someone whom people trust, respect, and yes, even love.

PSALMS 24 AND INVITING THE PRESENCE OF GOD INTO YOUR LIFE

> The earth and everything in it, the world and its inhabitants, belong to the Lord; for He laid its foundation on the seas and established it on the rivers. Who may ascend the mountain of the Lord? Who may stand in His holy place? The one who has clean hands and a pure heart, who has not set his mind on what is false, and who has not sworn deceitfully. He will receive blessing from the Lord, and righteousness from the God of his salvation. Such is the generation of those who seek Him, who seek the face of the God of Jacob. Selah Lift up your heads, you gates! Rise up, ancient doors! Then the King of glory will come in. Who is this King of glory? The Lord, strong and mighty, the Lord, mighty in battle. Lift up your heads, you gates! Rise up, ancient doors! Then the King of glory will come in. Who is He, this King of glory? The Lord of Hosts, He is the King of glory. Selah

When we worship and seek God with pure hearts and clean hands, recognizing that He is sovereign over everything, we invite His presence into our lives and our community. David writes of the mountain of the Lord, Jerusalem, the city surrounded by walls, whose gates are opened to receive the King of glory. But He will not be welcomed by those whose hands are not clean and whose hearts are not pure. That invites judgment, not the presence of God to bring blessing.

Men, you are the gates of your family. When you, as the leader of your family, give your worship to the Living God, making Him the priority of your life, when you live in obedience to Him, yearning to be acceptable to Him beyond all others, you are inviting the King of glory to enter the gates to your family. You are setting the example that has the most power to transform your family into a worshipping family, a godly family.

David was first and foremost a worshipper of God, and so must you be. David could say with the apostle Paul, "I want the men in every place to pray, lifting up holy hands" (1 Timothy 2:8). And men, when you do that, you change the world, beginning first with your families and spreading out to every area of your influence. Will you join with other men in every place and lift up holy hands?

QUESTIONS FOR REFLECTION

Personal Reflection

1. If you were to describe the biggest hurdle you face when it comes to privately or publicly giving God your worship, what would you highlight?

2. What do you think is the key to overcoming this hurdle?

3. What difference do you think it would make if you wrote out your praise to God first? If you gathered other men around you to worship together? If you asked your family members for ideas about how to worship together?

4. How does worship shape how you respond to difficult situations?

5. After reflecting on this chapter, how does your worship correspond to David's example?

Group Reflection

1. Does personal worship shape the way worship is experienced when gathered with other believers? Should it? How do they differ?

2. Should the motivation for worship be rooted in the character of God, the workings of God, or both? Are there other biblical motivations?

3. With David as the model, discuss how other biblical characters worshipped. Do you note any differences?

4. Should circumstances of life affect our worship?

Matt Surber is the lead pastor of Central Church in Collierville, Tennessee. Central Church was recently recognized as one of the top fifty fastest growing churches in Leadership Magazine and has a vision for a global gospel ministry impact through community ministry and church planting. Matt's undergraduate degree is from East Texas Baptist University. He attended Southwestern Theological Seminary as well as Trinity Evangelical Theological Seminary for graduate and postgraduate work. Matt has been married to his beautiful wife, Becky, for almost twenty years. They have two boys, Caleb and Josh, as well as a boxer named Camo. Matt is an avid sports nut and outdoorsman. He loves to spend time with his family and study churches.

www.ingramcontent.com/pod-product-compliance
Lightning Source LLC
Chambersburg PA
CBHW032032090426
42733CB00029B/356